W9-BNB-145

Thicker than Water

Essays by Adult
Siblings of People
with Disabilities

Edited by Don Meyer

Anderson County Library
Anderson, S.C.
AND

NO LONGER PROPERTY OF ANDERSON COUNTY LIBRARY

WOODBINE HOUSE • 2009

Photos on front and back covers courtesy of: Kitty Porterfield and John Burnett, Maryjane Westra and Martha Hartz, Sherry Gray and Suzy Gray, Zachary Rossetti and Todd Rossetti, and Emily Marino and Peter Marino.

© 2009 Don Meyer
First edition

All rights reserved. Published in the United States of America by Woodbine House, Inc., 6510 Bells Mill Rd., Bethesda, MD 20817. 800-843-7323. www.woodbinehouse.com

All proceeds to the editor from *Thicker Than Water* will benefit the Sibling Support Project.

Library of Congress Cataloging-in-Publication Data

Thicker than water : essays by adult siblings of people with disabilities / edited by Don Meyer.—1st ed.
   p. cm.
  ISBN 978-1-890627-91-1
  1. People with disabilities—Family relationships. 2. People with disabilities—Care. 3. Brothers and sisters. I. Meyer, Donald J. (Donald Joseph), 1951-
  HV1568.T46 2009
  362.4'043--dc22

                                                        2009007119

Manufactured in the United States of America

10 9 8 7 6 5 4 3 2 1

To George A. and Marion M. Wilson,
with gratitude

Table of Contents

Introduction

Marie had an epiphany.

In her forties, Marie had joined SibNet, my project's listserv for adult sibs of people who have disabilities. Her brother has autism.

Marie sought out SibNet because she's increasingly involved in her brother's life with each passing day. Her parents are not getting any younger and have been, at best, vague about their plans for her brother's future. And her brother's future is something that Marie thinks about a lot. She sought out SibNet because she felt a bit overwhelmed and needed a little support, some information, and a little validation.*

After reading other members' messages to SibNet for two weeks, Marie posted a note that read: *I have been on this list for a while now, and this is my first email to the group. I am so happy to have found Sib-*

---

* Over 95 percent of SibNet members are sisters. Just as daughters are more likely to care for aging parents than sons are, research indicates that sisters are more likely than brothers to be the point people in the lives of adults with disabilities when their parents no longer can. In many ways, adult sibling issues are women's issues.

Net! When I read your emails, it's like I am reading pages out of my own journal. I had no idea others have the ambivalent feelings I have about my brother. I am forty-something years old, and this is the first time I have ever shared my experiences with others who get it.

Forty years is a long time to wait for such validation.

Service providers would never make the parents of a child with special needs wait for forty years to meet other parents who have children with similar disabilities. But for some reason, this basic consideration isn't seen as important for brothers and sisters, many of whom will face the same issues and challenges as their parents at some point in their lives.

Brothers and sisters deserve better. They will, after all, be in the lives of their siblings who have disabilities longer than anyone—longer than any service provider or even their parents. In a relationship that may span up to eighty years, brothers and sisters will likely still be around when a favorite special education teacher is a distant memory and Mom and Dad are no longer available to be primary advocates.

Today's adult brothers and sisters already assume larger roles in the lives of people with disabilities than in previous generations, due to at least two converging social phenomena. First, because of advanced medical technologies, many people with disabilities now routinely outlive their parents. When parents pass away, and even as they age and become increasingly less able to care for their children with disabilities, siblings are often left to take on this role. Second, current social policies encourage people with disabilities to live and work in the community, but the funding to support programs that facilitate community integration is ever-diminishing. Currently, more than 70 percent of adults with intellectual disabilities remain at home after high school. At a time when service providers across the country struggle to help individuals with disabilities find housing and employment options, many adult siblings assume the *in loco parentis* roles previously played by the state.

Consequently, siblings of the baby boom and post-baby boom generations are called upon to be more involved than ever before in the lives of their brothers and sisters with disabilities—giving new meaning to the phrase "sandwich generation." Most will raise their own children, pursue their careers, look after their aging parents, and do whatever they can to ensure that their siblings with disabilities lead dignified lives living and working in the community. Call it, if you will (as adult siblings often do), life in the "club sandwich generation."

Brothers and sisters deserve respect for the many contributions they make to their families and to the lives of their siblings who have disabilities. They deserve understanding from parents and from service providers who profess to be interested in families, yet manage to overlook their unique concerns. And they deserve opportunities for basic considerations, such as validation and helpful information, for their benefit and to help them support their brothers and sisters.

But most of all, they deserve to know they are not alone.

In reading *Thicker Than Water,* brothers and sisters will meet other sibs who have had similar experiences; some, I am sure, for the first time. They'll develop a broader understanding of their own situation as authors share their views, concerns, and hard-earned joys. We hope our book will reach other audiences as well. Parents who read our book will surely think about their families in new ways as authors reflect on what their parents did to meet the needs of all family members, and what they wish their parents had done differently. And service providers, researchers, and policymakers who wish to create services that are truly family-centered and which take a comprehensive approach to enriching the lives of people with disabilities will learn about sibs' life-long and ever-changing joys, concerns, and contributions.

Please know that *Thicker Than Water* is <u>not</u> *Chicken Soup for the Sibling's Soul!* As you'll see, for some authors being the brother or sister of a person with special needs is a good thing, for others a not-so-good thing, and for many, something in-between. Consequently, readers will find that the authors' experiences are anything but monolithic. Some have found their experiences largely positive and even ennobling. Others have struggled mightily and have shared essays that read like modern versions of Dickens. For most contributors, however, it's a mixed bag: they have a deep, abiding love for their sibs who have disabilities, but it is a devotion that is never easy.

Essay authors were asked to comment on their lives growing up if they wished, but to primarily focus on here-and-now issues: What do you find yourself reflecting upon as you drive to work, take a shower, or mow the lawn? The essays are arranged in rough order of the contributors' ages to show readers how sibs' issues can change over time.

All of the authors—bless them—cheerfully agreed to be a part of this book, although many later noted what a difficult assignment it was. And, of course, they're right: is there a topic more subjective, personal, and elusive than the relationship one has with a brother or sister? How does one sum up the essence of a relationship so close to the bone in a few thousand words?

Regardless of the challenge, I am happy to report that the thirty-nine contributors have done a marvelous job of providing us with insight into one of life's richest, longest-lasting, and most complex relationships. I am grateful for their willingness to share their lives with us.

Don Meyer
Director, The Sibling Support Project
Seattle, Washington

1.
Asked and Answered

by Melissa Garrison

If you were to ask me my favorite question of all time, I know exactly what I would tell you: it would be "Sis? Can you be a bowl of chili?"

My brother, Brandon, woke me up with this question almost every day for three months, back in middle school. He heard someone mention a bowl of chili on *Sesame Street,* and it became an obsession. It was his great obsession and for three months, every morning, I woke up laughing. It was a lot better than his current obsession: listing every television show on every television channel in order by programming block. Not as amusing. Chili—especially *being* a bowl of chili—makes everything funnier, I guess.

Brandon's clinical diagnoses are autism, attention-deficit/hyperactivity disorder, and obsessive-compulsive disorder. When he was first diagnosed, the neurologist told my mother that he would never learn to talk. Now, at seventeen, you can't get him to *stop* talking. Brandon has a question for everything: you have to watch every word you say to him, because what you tell him determines which obsession he's going to respond with. I'll walk in the door and say, "Hey, Brandon!" and he'll reply, "Who says 'hey,' Sis?" Every time.

Brandon's life is built around these questions. They keep him safe. They order his world. They are his one line of communication with others. And they never stop.

Autism gave my brother a need for order, an overactive memory, perfect pitch, and an altered perspective of the world. It made him who he is. Autism did not steal his ability to interact with others, as physicians once predicted it would. It was obsessive-compulsive disorder that did that. It hijacked his ability to carry on a conversation without falling into a feedback loop. Everything, now, leads to a question.

Older, now—in my second year of college—I have some questions of my own—questions that might not prove so easily answered.

* * *

Brandon's crying. He opens the door to my room, sobbing, unable to speak, tears just streaming down his face.

"Brandon? What's wrong?" I jump up. I hug him. I wipe his face. He cannot answer me.

I run upstairs and tell my mother that he's crying, and ask if she knows why.

"He misses you," she says. "You're never home."

At twenty, I've been looking at apartments of my own—and I feel the most incredible sense of guilt and shame. What audacity must I have, thinking about leaving my brother? How can I leave home? He counts on me being there, to say good night to him. I'm a part of the routine— probably expendable, given time—but who wants to find out for sure?

Even if I know I have to, how do I leave my brother behind?

* * *

Brandon's and my biological father has always hated Brandon's "disability." When Brandon was just a baby, he suggested putting him into an institution, so our family could be spared the "impossibility" of raising him. "If there's a God, why would he give me a monster like this for a child?" he would ask. "I should have drowned him when he was an infant." He has been out of our lives, off and on, for thirteen years, now—but, every so often, he rears his ugly head. He writes horrible letters about Brandon and says terrible things about him in court. Sometimes, when I read particularly virulent hate mail from him, I think about the future, and feel afraid—if my mother and stepfather died, who would get Brandon? Could *he* get Brandon? What would he *do* with Brandon, if he had him? How can I prevent that from happening?

* * *

Brandon is screaming. He's pounding on the walls, because I've re-fused to list the game shows and their hosts for the third time this evening. I'm watching him, and I realize: I don't know how to talk to you any more. *When did I lose that?*

* * *

Yeah, here and there, things get rough. Everyone knows that life is hard. But the strange thing about sharing your life with some-one—not just a person with a disability, but *anyone*—is that for ev-ery one of the arguments and hardships and unanswerable questions, there are at least two moments of absolute joy.

* * *

I'm sitting on the couch with a friend, watching television. It's about nine p.m. Brandon wanders out into the living room to say good night—naked.

"Brandon! Put your clothes on!" *I shout.*

"Why, Sis?"

"Because you don't just walk out in front of company naked, that's why."

"Sis?"

"Yes?"

"Do you know all the characters that wear clothes?"

I steer him back to his bedroom, closing the door behind him. "What was that about?" my friend asks. How do I explain that? Moreover, even though I know it wasn't funny, how do I fight the urge to laugh?

* * *

We're sitting on the floor, playing Disney Scene It? *on the TV. Our parents are gone for the afternoon. It's an easy question: one I know he knows the answer to. "Question: Which Disney characters sang the hit Disney song, 'A Whole New World?'"*

"Aladdin and Jasmine." It's immediate. He's grinning.

"YES!" High-five. I laugh. "That's an easy one, huh?"

He flaps. I love when he flaps. It means he's excited. He laughs, and then he smiles at me. "Sis?"

"Yeah, dude?"

"Do we love Disney Scene It?*"*

I know what he means. "Oh, yeah. I love it, too."

He laughs again, and his smile is so beautiful that it makes me feel golden inside.

* * *

Brandon and I have gone to the movies, to see Alvin and the Chipmunks. I remember first taking him to the movies, back when he was seven or eight, and being nervous about his behavior: he would talk, he would shout, he would stand up and pull up his underwear in the middle of the movie. We never knew how he was going to respond.

Today, he is absolutely perfect. He shares his popcorn with me. He laughs, that laugh that I know stems from genuine amusement. At the end of the show, he applauds. "Great show!" he says, over and over. "Great show!"

As we're walking across the parking lot, I take his hand, and he turns to look at me. What he says next absolutely astonishes me:

"Sis?" he asks. "Did you like that movie?"

No subtext, no underlying obsession. An honest question.
I put my arm around his shoulder. "Yeah, dude," I say. "I really did."
"What was your favorite part?"
And I tell him.

* * *

And then there are moments of absolute brilliance. Brandon will ask me a question about the Children's Institute, where he used to go for therapy when he was four years old—he remembers every detail. Or he will put a twenty-year-old Nintendo cartridge into our old system and play through the entire game without losing a life, even though he hasn't seen the game since he was three and a half. Or we will go to the theatre to see a movie, and the first thing he'll do when we get home is go down and play the score on the piano, although he's never taken a single lesson. Sometimes, when things like this happen, I don't know quite what to think. I'll stand behind him and watch him, quietly, and wonder, *Where did you come from?*

* * *

Things have become more difficult since I graduated high school. I'm not around as much as I used to be. It's hard to "find time" to talk to my family. Brandon tends to take the back seat to my other commitments, which is wrong of me, but sometimes I don't feel as if I have any other choice. My mom tells me that "charity begins at home," and that before I go out trying to save the world I should consider my own brother. She's right. But sometimes, I don't. I feel like we've grown apart, over time, Brandon and I. I wonder how to reach him.

And then we'll play a board game, or go to a movie. And I remember something very simple: Brandon is my shining star. His talents change people's lives. His smile lights up the hearts of everyone around him. He has taught me patience, even though I sometimes forget to practice it. He has taught me acceptance and the value of difference. These are lessons that I will cherish for the rest of my life.

And there are some things he hasn't taught me—things I'll have to learn on my own. Some questions may take a long time for me to answer. Some of my questions might *never* be answered.

And that's okay, too. Because, if nothing else, Brandon has shown me that love never fails. There is *always* a way back home: I will never lose him.

And even if some of my questions remain unanswered, I'll always know how to imitate a bowl of chili. I wonder whether, in its own way, that may be the most important thing of all.

* * *

Melissa Garrison *is a sophomore at the University of Washington, where she's cycled through majors in biology, sociology, psychology, social welfare, English, anthropology, and drama in the last six quarters. When she's not trying to choose a major, she's either at the* Rocky Horror Picture Show, *putting chocolate-chip-mint face paint on a mime, acting, writing short fiction, knitting, crocheting, reading, trying (and failing) to learn to play a musical instrument, or doing what she loves most: advocating for the disabled and GBLT communities. In the future, she expects to find herself in an inner-city condo with her brother, a girlfriend/boyfriend, a Harley, a small library, and way more yarn than she can actually justify possessing. She thinks that doing strange things in the name of art is a beautiful thing. In 2004, Melissa and her brother Brandon were featured in a story about sibling issues on ABC's* 20/20.

2.
It All Changes and Stays the Same

Matt Kramer

Lying in my bed awake at night as a child in elementary school, I often read books late into the night. My brother Mike would yell something at me, and I'd yell back. We'd fight over stupid things, like who was friends with whom, and what girls we liked. It was not unusual for someone to throw a pillow or two. Eventually, Mike would get tired and go to sleep, at which point I heckled him to keep him awake until he could not stay awake any longer.

More than once, I would hear a strange sound coming from Mike's bed. I'd sit up and turn to see him shaking and breathing oddly. He was having seizures. I'd scream for our parents to come and check on him. Mom and Dad would come down; sometimes they'd realize that Mike was OK, other times, they determined that he needed medication. In either case, it was a good thing I was able to get someone's attention. I shudder to think what may have happened had I not been able to alert them.

Today, Mike and I have much the same relationship as we did back then. We still fight a lot about anything one could think of.

We fight about what we are going to watch on TV, and who is going to take care of our dog, and whose turn it is on one of our entertainment systems. We frequently go to Starbucks together for coffee. Although the meetings are enjoyable, there is, of course, bickering. When one of us gets ahead of the other, he will chant something like "slowpoke" to the person behind. We occasionally push and shove each other if we get angry at something the other says. Mike gets angry with me when I question him about where he is going when he leaves the house, and I get angry with him when he refuses to answer my questions, or if he screams at every little thing I do.

At the same time, we look out for each other, much as we did as children. Mike usually, though not always willingly, picks something up if I drop it. He helps out with other things I cannot do. He walks our dog, which is something I cannot really do with my wheelchair. Sometimes the battery for my chair stops working, leaving me to push my heavy chair by myself. When this happens, Mike comes up behind me and pushes me when I need it.

He also cares when I am sick or in the hospital. When I had a fever last week, he asked me every single day if I was feeling better. Though I often said no, I appreciated his asking. He did things that I would normally do such as giving the cat food and water, or going upstairs to get something I needed. He also is aware of my difficulty in getting around the community sometimes, and frequently offers to pick up my prescriptions.

For my part, I feel pretty protective of my Mike. I point out things that he should be aware of or doesn't always recognize, like people who tease him or might take advantage of him. I am pretty hard on him if he misbehaves towards me or anyone else. I always feel a bit like an older brother, even though we are twins. I bicker with him sometimes just because I feel like doing so, but more often I bicker with him to get him to behave—as hard as that may be sometimes. He has made tremendous progress in this respect throughout the years, but still gets on people's nerves and needs a good yelling from his "older brother" twin on occasion.

Though we fight a lot, it is clear that Mike and I care about each other, especially when push comes to shove. Neither of us would ever tell the other one how much, but our actions (my monitoring of him at night and his assisting me in my daily needs) speak louder than our bickering words. We are brothers, with all that comes with that label. I definitely see both of us moving out of our parents' house in the not-too-distant future. We are both too independent to stay here all our lives. Though we will not live in the same place, I suspect we will be calling each other often, and will fight and care about each other for the rest of our lives.

* * *

Matt Kramer *lives in Minnesota and is a graduate of Lyon College with a B.A. in English. Currently looking for employment, Matt hopes to work in the field of public policy. He volunteers at the local Courage Center, and is interested in politics and the effect they have on people with disabilities. When not volunteering, he likes writing about his life experiences, and reading about politics as well as disabilities. He enjoys many different types of music, including classic rock, modern rock, and folk. He played adaptive sports in high school, and continues to have friendships with his former teammates. He is hoping to use his life experiences to help younger people with disabilities learn how to advocate effectively on their own behalf. Matt's brother John wrote the essay "I Am Not My Brother's Keeper" found on page 20.*

3.
Katie

Matthew Carpenter

It has been fourteen years since I last wrote about my relationship with my younger sister Katie. During this time many things have happened—we are now both adults, we have both studied at college, and we no longer live at home with our parents. I am now twenty-seven, and Katie is twenty-three.

Katie was adopted into the Carpenter family when I was four years old. When I was younger my parents made sure I was an active part of Katie's life, so that I would have the skills to be a successful older brother. My parents taught me some sign language, which allowed us to communicate from an early age. They explained Katie's educational and medical needs, which helped me understand Down syndrome and Katie. Because of this, I wasn't dogged with misconceptions, prejudice, or jealousy and this laid the foundation for the relationship we have today.

Katie is now an adult, leading an adult life. Thanks to the efforts of my parents, Katie goes to a residential college and lives independent of our family in a shared house. As her older brother, I have always been very protective of Katie, almost to a point of paranoia. I have always worried that people will take advantage of her, even if it's something as simple as talking to her the wrong way, or giving her too little—or even too much—attention. Over time, Katie has taught me that I needn't worry. Katie is happy, and how other people act toward her is their concern, not hers.

Several years ago, I took Katie back to college for the third term of her first year. When we arrived at the campus, Katie told me where to park, opened her front door, directed me to help her unpack, and then made us a cup of tea. After I had finished the tea, we said our goodbyes and she showed me back to the car. That was it—no checking in with a supervisor or housemother, no "welcome back" event. I remember feeling utterly astounded by this experience. I stopped at the end of the drive to the college and phoned my mother. I asked "Who is looking after her? No one knows she's here!" In the end it was fine—that's how the college works. They give their students many opportunities for independence and Katie has thrived in this environment. But that event has never left me. And it changed my ideas about what Katie is capable of.

Maintaining communication with Katie can be very difficult. Katie speaks with a unique speech pattern, which she supports with simple sign language and gestures. You have to have a keen ear to differentiate between similar-sounding words. As soon as I left home, my ability to easily understand what Katie says quickly decreased. I frequently have to ask Katie to repeat herself. Ironically, it hasn't been a detriment to our relationship. My inability to easily understand her is now a part of our natural banter and she teases me about it. Katie has learned to use different words when I can't understand her and it's improved our communication—and her vocabulary. Still, I find it difficult to speak to Katie on the phone. We both need to concentrate fully when we talk, and this is hard to do over the phone.

During her third year at college, Katie gave me a few "prank" phone calls. These calls usually included a lot of giggling and the occasional swear word. It was funny to begin with, but when the calls became a bit too frequent, we removed my number from her mobile phone. I have recently put my number back into Katie's phone and I have had more luck communicating with her by text messages—another surprising revelation. Now that the prank calls have subsided, I enjoy her occasional calls. Last Saturday she called me at seven-thirty in the morning to tell me she was going to watch a musical in London. She was extremely excited. Despite her timing, I was really pleased that she called. Having Katie call her big brother to share a joyous occasion felt like a milestone.

When Katie and I meet in person, it is much easier to communicate. We still discuss the things we have been discussing for years: *Eastenders* (a British soap opera), what music we like, and which one of us is the naughtiest. (I claim to win, but she always trumps me with the "toast in the VCR" incident.) There can be weeks between these meetings, and even though we fall into our usual banter in short order, it can be strained at first. The amount of contact Katie and I have concerns me. Communication is the lifeblood of any healthy relationship, and currently I am reliant on my parents and our younger sister, Grace, to keep in touch with Katie. As I look to the future, I know this is an issue I will need to resolve.

When we lived together, Katie's behavior could be extremely challenging with bouts of temper. We would argue over who had the TV remote and other trivial things; our arguments seemed to escalate very quickly. When I was in my late teens, Katie's stubbornness was at its peak. Although she too was a teenager, she would sit on the floor and cry if she didn't get her way. I vividly remember an outburst in the middle of a shopping mall. She sat on the floor and screamed because we were leaving and she wanted to stay. I can still picture the looks people gave me as I tried to calm her but only succeeded in making matters worse. It was an extremely embarrassing situation. In adulthood, Katie's behavior is much better—she's much calmer and easier to reason with. As a result, we are calmer with one another and a more mature relationship has developed.

I love being Katie's brother, even though I feel guilty sometimes that I am not a bigger part of her life. In writing this essay I have realized that I still have a significant role for Katie. She is an independent young woman who has an older brother who is devoted to her. I think she knows that if she ever needs me, I will be there for her. And when she doesn't, I will be happy to see her enjoying her life.

* * *

Matthew Carpenter *is twenty-seven years old and lives on the outskirts of Birmingham, England with his wife, Anna. His younger sister Katie, the subject of this essay, is just turning twenty-four and lives in a village about twenty minutes' drive from his house. His parents and youngest sister also live close by. Mat has a degree in Genetics and qualified as a teacher in 2002. He is currently the head of a science department in a challenging inner city high school. He has always been committed to working with young people and enriching their lives, especially through science. Both of his parents work in education and have been a constant source of inspiration. He enjoys being outside, whether it's gardening, mountain biking, or walking his two Springer Spaniels, Tilly and Meg. Mat likes watching soccer and rugby, but isn't very good at either of them.*

4.
Driving Forward

Brian Skotko

I could see her in the distance—Kristin, my sister with Down syndrome, had just emerged from our local craft store's warehouse where she had completed her first day of work as a packager. She was standing outside the entrance, purse in hand, waiting for the taxi that my parents had arranged to take her back home. And there I was, parked surreptitiously in my dated gray Oldsmobile behind the giant conifer in the parking lot. I felt like I was part of an action thriller, but this plot was to take a turn that I would never have anticipated.

I remember the day when Kristin beamed over the phone that she had nabbed a job (with my parents' help) at the craft store. We were all excited. Kristin—who had worked so hard during high school and endured, in many ways, an educational system that was not as advanced as her own hopes and dreams—had landed a job just like everyone else. She, too, could look forward to lunchroom chats, paycheck arrivals, and the sound feeling of purpose. I was home briefly from college that summer, making the final preparations for an internship in Washington, D.C. Having experienced the randomness and danger of taxi riding throughout the country, I asked my parents, in private: Would you like me to follow Kristin's cab home for at least the first couple of days to make sure that things go smoothly?

My parents thought it was a great idea. My father would be dropping Kristin off at work in the morning, en route to his own office. But, both my father and mother would still be at work when Kristin's shift ended. So, they had arranged for a local cab service to drive Kristin home from work each day. She already knew the security code to our house, and she certainly knew how to take care of herself at home. I was just concerned: would she make it home safely? Could we trust a random stranger to drive my sister home?

So, there I was waiting and watching. And, the moment did come when a blue-and-white paneled cab pulled up, and Kristin got in. They were off, but not me. I waited for two cars—just like I had seen in the movies—to pull out between the cab and my car. I would leave no chance for getting caught.

But, then it happened: the cab driver took a left at an intersection where he should have gone straight. I followed. Then, they pulled into an abandoned housing development. Where were they going? What was I supposed to do? My mind was racing with the possibilities: Ram my car into theirs? Call 9-1-1? Honk madly? Before I could decide, they pulled into the driveway of one of the houses, and I pulled into the driveway across the street. As I was opening my driver's door, preparatory to running across the street and rescuing my sister, the cab started to back up. I jumped back in my car and continued the chase. This time, they went straight home; Kristin got out of the car and let herself into our home.

Not to blow my cover, I continued to circle the development for a few more minutes before returning home with the announcement, "Hey, Kristin, I'm home—back from some errands." I asked Kristin how her day had been, and her one-word responses did not reveal any difficulties. So, I asked directly, "Did the cab get lost at all coming home?"

"Yes," she responded.

"How did he finally figure things out?" I queried. Kristin then pulled from her purse the laminated directions my parents had made for her and explained how she had given these instructions to the cab driver. She was, in the most complete sense, resourceful.

But, I could not take any more chances. The next day around 2:45 p.m., there I was again, idling in my gray jalopy waiting for the cab driver to pick up my sister. He was prompt. She got in, and in my carefully calibrated scheme, I followed, leaving no less than two cars between me and my sister. She went directly home. I circled the block and again announced that I had arrived home after running some errands.

On the third day, as I was staring at the evergreen, I had decided that this would probably be enough. Three data points were enough to draw conclusions that my sister would be safe. If I followed just this last time and there were no hitches, I could let my parents know that the experiment had worked. So, I followed again, as Kristin made her way home after another fulfilling day at work.

At the first intersection, however, the two cars separating us peeled off, making right turns, placing me directly behind the cab as we continued straight on the main road. I could see the back of my sister's head and imagined what she must be feeling: scared a bit, being driven by a stranger? Tired, perhaps, after a full day of work?

No. At the stop sign, my sister turned around and waved to me, smiling—or was she laughing? She had known all along that her big brother was crazy, following the cab home after work each day. I was too concerned and had failed to believe in her full potential. At a time when she needed a big brother, I was second-guessing her own independence. But, she knew that, and she had allowed me to be worried. She had yet again taught me a life lesson about growing up as an adult sibling and learning to let go.

I am one of three adult children; and as my sister Allison, aged twenty-five, and I, aged twenty-nine, think about our relationship with Kristin, now twenty-seven, I find that I continue to worry about several life items. At the same time, I try to remember—and implement—the taxi lesson that I learned from Kristin as I find myself thinking about the following:

Where will my sister live in the untoward event that some disaster should strike both of my parents? In many ways, I feel lucky. My wife, Carrie, and I would both welcome Kristin into our home in Massachusetts should anything happen to my parents. My sister, Allison, and her husband, Matthew, have also said that Kristin could live with them in Indiana. But, Kristin lives in Ohio right now with my parents, and her entire world is in Ohio. Her jobs, her friends, her doctors, her extracurriculars—they're all local. Kristin could certainly live in Massachusetts or Indiana, but is that what she wants? And, would that be the best move for her?

My parents have always encouraged us to ask questions about Kristin. So, all of us, including Kristin, are starting to have conversations about her future. And, we're taking advantage of the many resources that already exist. We downloaded, for free, a fill-in-the-blanks Letter of Intent assembled by Jo Ann Simons, the mother of a young adult with Down syndrome. (The document is called "Footprints for the Future" and can be found under "Resources" at www. theemarc.org.) We've also read *The Special Needs Planning Guide*, by John Nadworny and Cynthia Haddad. And, my parents are attending workshops on transition planning at the National Down Syndrome Congress's annual workshops.

Is my sister's job fulfilling to her? Research has shown that people with disabilities make excellent employees—reliable, timely, dedicated. And yet, workers with disabilities are often the first to be fired. Such has been the case with my sister, who no longer works at the craft store because of "downsizing." My parents have been resourceful in putting together part-time jobs, but Kristin is becoming increasingly bored at work. The jobs were chosen for her, out of lack of options, and she has settled into routines. She does not talk about work as much, no longer eager to spread the office gossip—perhaps, because she is not included in such conversations.

Again, my sister and I—along with our spouses—have mentioned our observations to our parents, and they have taken action. They are looking, with Kristin, for new opportunities in Cleveland. This hunt for meaningful employment will be a lifelong one, but I know that we are not alone. Many other families have similar concerns, and we are connecting with them and taking their advice.

Will my sister be able to love the way she wants to love? The year 2007 was a fun one for the Skotkos: Allison and Matthew got married two months after Carrie and I did. You bet that Kristin played an essential bridesmaid role in both ceremonies, not to mention her leading dynamism on the dance floor. But, what relationships does the future hold for her? She has a long-time boyfriend, but she also talks about her future with Clay Aiken, her American idol. She goes on dates, supervised, but what will happen if and when she wants to have more independence with her own intimacies?

In many ways, such contemplation is an inherently uncomfortable one. No one really likes to think about the love life of their other family members, but when you have an adult sibling with Down syndrome, that somehow changes, a bit. My interests center around her happiness—wanting her to know love in a way that makes her happy, whatever form that might take. Terri Couwenhoven, in her book, *Teaching Children with Down Syndrome about Their Bodies, Boundaries, and Sexuality,* and Leslie Walker Hirsh, in her workshops on sexuality for people with intellectual disabilities, challenge all of us to think outside of the box.

And we will. And Kristin will. Kristin will continue to show us all how to laugh when others are frowning, how to dance when others are sitting in the corner, how to keep trying when we have still not gotten it right on the third or fourth tries. Kristin will continue to be a life coach, defining me, calibrating me, inspiring me. I know that she has given me gifts that I could never repay over a lifetime, no matter how hard I try. Even my career as a geneticist, doing research on Down syndrome and working directly with children who have Down syndrome, will be insufficient. I am and will always be a better person because of Kristin.

So, as Allison, Kristin, and I all continue to grow older, I know that our sibling relationships will evolve, accommodating life's emotional advances. But, I also know that one thing will always remain steadfast: we will continue to love Kristin with an unyielding completeness.

* * *

Brian Skotko, M.D., M.P.P., *a resident physician at Children's Hospital Boston and Boston Medical Center, coauthored the national award-winning book,* Common Threads: Celebrating Life with Down Syndrome. *He is also the co-author, with Sue Levine, of* Fasten Your Seatbelt: A Crash Course on Down Syndrome for Brothers and Sisters. *He is a graduate of Duke University, Harvard Medical School, and Harvard's John F. Kennedy School of Government. Brian recently authored major research on how physicians deliver a diagnosis of Down syndrome to new and expectant parents. He has been featured in* The Wall Street Journal, The New York Times, The Washington Post, The L.A. Times, *NPR's* On Point, *and* ABC's Good Morning America. *Brian serves on the Board of Directors for the Massachusetts Down Syndrome Congress and the National Down Syndrome Society. He further serves on the Professional Advisory Council to the National Down Syndrome Congress.*

5.
I Am Not My Brother's Keeper

John Kramer

"**M**om, I'm sure he is fine. I am on the Blue Line and his flight just landed. I will be there in twenty minutes."

I was excited. My brother was coming to visit me in Chicago for the first time ever by himself. I thought, *He can do this…he is so obsessive about details…he knows what to do.*

"Yes Mom, I know. I am almost there. I will let you know the second I get to him."

Seven minutes later: "Hello? Yes, Mom, I am almost to baggage claim. He just called…right…I know. We're supposed to meet there."

"Mom, I am in baggage claim. I will find him. I haven't even been here thirty seconds yet."

Boy, am I gonna get it if I am wrong about this, I thought.

Was Mom overreacting? No, not really. The situation seemed made for Murphy's Law. I worried a bit that Mike might have a seizure or something worse, but ended up giving Mike two basic instructions: 1) meet me at the baggage claim; and 2) if you get lost, seek help from someone in a uniform.

It turns out that the only glitch Mike and I had that day at O'Hare was that he thought I was driving, so he waited curbside looking for my Mazda. Not bad for a first time flying alone to one of the world's busiest airports.

What it all really came down to was chance. Mike and I wanted to take the chance that Mike could fly on his own. Mom? Well, in this case she got overruled. Maybe we got lucky, but maybe it was something else....

I am the older brother of twins who both have developmental disabilities. Mike has been labeled as having cerebral palsy, an intellectual disability, Pervasive Developmental Disorder Not Otherwise Specified (a.k.a. PDD-NOS), and a seizure disorder. Matt has been labeled as having spina bifida and a nonverbal learning disability. Mike wasn't expected to walk or talk. Neither was expected to live much past twenty. In the early days, the doctors were wrong on almost all counts.

Mike's trip to Chicago was one of the first occasions I noticed real differences regarding how I feel about my brothers and what my parents feel. While this might sound like I have a confrontational relationship with my parents, nothing could be further from the truth. But those differences are still there.

An obvious issue is that I am not in a good position to know a lot about my brothers' daily lives; I only see them a handful of times a year. When I talk to them on the phone, Mike tells me all the Twins scores, and Matt and I don't get much deeper than discussions about politics, music, and the latest article in *The Onion*. For years now, I have lived hundreds of miles away from them; consequently, I don't provide much support to Mom and Dad.

My lack of day-to-day interaction with my brothers wrestles with my desire to give them independent lives. On one hand, I think: How do I—as someone who currently sees Mike less than three weeks out of the year—dare to think that I know his abilities and limitations better than my parents? But on the other hand, I ask myself: Why am I even thinking about whether my twenty-four-year-old brother can fly by himself? He is not the person I knew twelve years ago. If he were, I never would have thought he could attempt to do this on his own.

But for me, the hardest issue is one that gets very little play. There's much talk among professionals interested in sibling support regarding how typically developing sibs sometimes feel "left out" of aspects of family life and parents' attention because of the needs of their brothers and sisters. While that may be true, few of us consider whether or not people with disabilities want things that way. My guess is that if they had their way, most people with disabilities would rather not be the suns in their families' solar systems. Also, most of us rarely consider people with disabilities in their capacity as brothers and sisters, with their own take on their families. Most of us—myself included—don't always consider how perceptive people with disabilities can be about their families.

And it makes me wonder: if sibs without disabilities complain about a lack of parental attention, do people with disabilities complain about *too much* attention?

I'm sure my brothers knew growing up—and certainly know now—that Mom and Dad spent more time with them because they *had* to. And I know nondisabled siblings know this, too—it's no secret. But what's never discussed is what do people with disabilities think of all this attention?

I think researchers, experts, and even other siblings often miss the boat. It is not that people with disabilities get more attention than their brothers and sisters: it's the *type* of attention they get that is different. This attention makes their lives profoundly different than ours—and it can contribute to isolation. This realization was not something that I arrived at overnight, but over years of experiences with my brothers. Here's one example, taken from a typical holiday event at the Kramer house:

"Where's Matt?" my wife would say.

"He's in his room, watching TV," I'd reply.

"Why is he doing that? We're all sitting here talking...MATT!"

A couple days later, I asked him why he didn't join us. His reply was something along the lines of, "Oh, I didn't know what you guys were doing; I thought you just wanted to be with each other." He isolated himself because he thought that his presence was an imposition.

When my wife asked Matt if he wanted to go out with me and my friends for my birthday, he was shocked. I don't blame him. I had never asked him to hang out with my friends. It was never a conscious thing; it just didn't occur to me to do so.

Who knows how long my brothers and I have had this mindset? Perhaps parts of us have never progressed past our teenage years. Or maybe I just don't know my brothers so well after all. Perhaps the distance really has rendered me clueless about what they are really like.

But how well do they know me? I recently heard through the grapevine that one of my brothers—Matt, I think—noted that I was the "perfect kid" and that I "never did anything wrong." I thought, wow, my brother really doesn't know me! Matt, did you ever hear about the time I emptied a five-gallon container of gasoline in our parents' car trunk? That one took months to address. Or how about the time I scratched the entire length of Dad's car with my bike handle? If not, you have now! My brother evidently does not recall these little episodes.

Disability is ever-present in our family, but it is only *part* of what we're all about. It wasn't until recently that I asked my own brothers what it was like to have a disability. Who knows why we avoided the topic for so long? Maybe it was too hard to talk about. Maybe we just were being guys and preferred to keep the talk to "guy stuff." More likely, it was just that their disabilities were a "given." Regardless, one day I decided I didn't know enough about their experiences. So I asked. I felt a little like a psychologist trying to analyze his own family—yikes! I didn't let that stop me, though. I needed to listen. I needed to stop being a big brother and to just be a brother. I took a chance, sat down, and listened.

After a bumpy start, our conversation eventually meandered into disability oppression—certainly not a dinner-table topic in our family. But what they said amazed me, and a whole different world opened up to me. "Yeah, I notice it," Mike said when I asked him if people bug him or tease him about his disability. "Oh yeah, it's pretty uncomfortable," Matt agreed. When I asked them what they did in those situations Mike said, "I just walk away from it." They both recounted years of stories from school ranging from feeling isolated to being made fun of. They weren't crying about it, or even particularly angry—it just was the way it was. The conversation lasted a couple hours until Mike left to go to work and Matt and I drifted on to other topics.

The conversation has been revisited over the years—especially by Matt, voicing his concern about people taking advantage of Mike. Granted, most of the time we still talk about the Minnesota Vikings, or the latest Minnesota Twin to be traded away, or the weather in whatever cities we're in, but I'm very grateful that I took that chance that day and I would like to think that it opened up a different chapter in our brotherhood.

* * *

"Hey Matt, are you ready?" I asked.

"Yeah, come on in," Matt opened the apartment door. He was visiting me in Chicago, but staying with our friend, as my apartment was inaccessible to wheelchairs.

"John, I will pay you," Matt said to me when I was providing care for him. I thought: *This is great—when he pays for his supports, he has control and does not have to rely solely on the goodwill of others.*

But I told him, "Of course not. Matt, you are my guest here in Chicago and I am really glad you came." I began to wonder if he worried about Mom and Dad taking care of him for so many years. I began to wonder what Matt's next step will be. I am not there to help with his care. Mom and Dad will not always be. What's next for us all?

* * *

No matter how much support I may one day provide, it won't be the same as the support Matt and Mike get from Mom and Dad. There is something different about being a sibling—a different perception. Maybe part of it is that we are not as protective; we are more willing to let our brothers and sisters take chances. Honestly, maybe part of it is that siblings are too busy with their own families and careers and just don't have the time to monitor their siblings. And maybe siblings are—consciously or unconsciously—aware of just how long-lasting, constant, and ever-changing their relationships will be with their sibs who have disabilities and so they take a longer view than moms and dads.

I will likely know my brothers a lot longer than my parents will, so I want to keep up with them—what they are doing, and who they are. And I've come to realize that I don't really know as much about them as I thought I did. That's okay. We've got a lot of time.

I have learned that disability affects all members of our family, but it is not the sum total of who we are. I have also learned to expect the unexpected—and that the unexpected certainly is not always roses. Regardless, the unexpected is the only constant in life.

* * *

"Hi Mike, I am over here. How was your flight?"

The airport's automatic door did its best to shut before Mike got through the door. It failed. The sounds of honking horns and slamming trunks filled the summer air.

"Oh. Hi John. I thought you were driving. I was looking for your car."

"No problem, Mike. Can I grab one of your bags?"

"Sure."

"Have you ever been on the El Train before?"

"No."

"Come on, let's go. How have you been?"

* * *

John Kramer is currently a Ph.D. candidate in Disability Studies who works in the Rehabilitation Research and Training Center on Aging with Developmental Disabilities at the University of Illinois at Chicago. His current work focuses on the roles that siblings with and without disabilities play in each other's lives in planning for the future when parents can no longer provide care. John is also one of the founding members of the Sibling Leadership Network and Supporting Illinois Brothers and Sisters. John received his M.A. from the University of Chicago in 2002. His master's thesis was on perceived differential treatment experienced by siblings of children with autism. John is also the older brother of two young men with disabilities who are twins. One of the twins, Matt, is the author of "It All Changes and Stays the Same," page 7. John's brothers continue to be contributors to a fulfilling, rich, and happy family life.

6.
What Was I Thinking!!

Kay Swanson

Wow, what I have I gotten myself into? I thought. Our son, John, was less than two months old and daughter, Katie, was two years old, and my sister, Beth, was coming to stay with us while my parents went on a business trip. I am Beth's only sibling, and she'd always stayed with us when my parents traveled. Being with us, at our home, is Beth's idea of vacation. Even though I'm still up all night with kids, and busy chasing Katie, it was hard to say no.

My friends thought I was crazy to add a sister with autism—and her two dogs—to the craziness that accompanies newborns and toddlers. Because she has trouble with transitions, the first twenty-four hours with Beth are always trying. She often has meltdowns and we both end up frustrated. I wasn't sure if I would have the energy. This trip, I hoped, would be different. . . .

In the end, the trip *was* different. Beth learned to adjust to baby John's crying much better than she had with Katie. Beth has sensory issues and can only tolerate a certain amount of noise. Meltdowns, similar to a toddler's tantrums, were minimal on this trip.

Beth was OK that the bedroom that was once hers was now painted pink and turned into Katie's room. Luckily, we were still able to give Beth a room of her own, as she likes to watch her favorite TV shows on her old VCR tapes at all hours of the day and night. She definitely needs her space.

Beth has visited us for ten years. She can read, write, talk, take care of her own personal hygiene, and prepare some of her own meals. I was grateful for this independence during her most recent visit, as I was busy caring for my two little ones. She was helpful with Katie, although I think Katie's occasional typical two-year-old tantrums scared her. She loved holding baby John and gave me some much needed-time to grab a shower or cook or clean.

Beth and I don't get out as much as we used to. The dynamics of her visits have changed. We used to do carefree sisterly activities like shopping and going out to lunch. These days we eat quickly and avoiding shopping trips altogether unless Don is home to watch the kids.

During her last visit, Don took Katie and Beth to play mini golf. Katie loved it even though Beth tried to reason with Katie about how to play the game. At two, Katie didn't care! And Beth bought Katie a Slip-and-Slide, but in truth, she wanted to use it herself! Our backyard was prefect for it and everyone had lots of fun.

Over the years, people have asked me what it is like to have a sister with a disability, but the truth is it's the only life I know. I look at other sibling relationships and try to understand them—but it is difficult. I've never fully experienced the ups and downs of a "typical" sibling relationship. These days, my relationship with Beth is that of an older sibling even though she's two years older than I am. Our mental age gap has increased over the years.

Finding a husband who would love and accept Beth for who she is was a challenge and I am thankful I found Don. But the merging of the families hasn't been perfect. I tried to be open about Beth with my in-laws, but it just didn't work. They are kind to her but they do not seem to see why Beth's future is a priority of mine. Consequently, I avoid talking with them about my sister and the issues I face as a sibling.

One of my pet peeves is when a friend, family member, or acquaintance tells me they "understand" my situation with my sister. Unless they have a sibling with a disability, they have no clue what it is like. There is no amount of reading they can do to begin to comprehend the many complicated and lifelong issues that go with having a sibling with special needs. I prefer for people to try to listen to me and to tell me they are doing their best to empathize and comprehend my concerns. My husband, my parents, and my close friends have been great about this.

As Don and I think about future visits—and the possibility of Beth living with us—we realize we will need to accommodate Beth's often-challenging behaviors. She is frequently anxious and her schedule rules her life. Beth is clinically depressed and her anxiety has been difficult to treat. She sees a psychiatrist at least twice each year to evaluate her anxiety and depression and to discuss her medication. If Beth doesn't like someone, she can be very rude. She remembers everything, including past arguments with people. Bygones are rarely bygones. It's life as I know it.

Because of my experiences with Beth—and because I'm a special education teacher—I am often asked what parents and service providers can do to help siblings. I'd encourage any service provider who is interested in families to start a Sibshop. They're wonderful, and participants have a great time hanging out with a great group of kids! I wish they were available when I was younger.

All in all, Beth is doing well adapting to the changes in our ever-evolving family. I'm glad Beth likes little kids. If she didn't, I'd have a whole different set of challenges to face. Although I was unaware of it at the time, growing up with Beth taught me patience, acceptance, and understanding. It's my hope that Beth will teach my kids the same lessons. The possibility that my kids may have guardianship of Beth someday is always in the back of my mind. While I'd rather not think of this possibility when Katie's only two and Beth is thirty-six, it's still there.

* * *

Kay Swanson *lives with her husband, Don, and children, Katie and John, in a suburb of Atlanta, Georgia. She's a full-time elementary special education teacher for Cobb County Public Schools and is a sibling advisor for the Georgia Sensory Assistance Project. Kay received the Teacher of the Year award from the Georgia Sensory Assistance Project in 2004 for her work with students with vision and hearing impairments and her work with siblings by conducting Sibshops. As many of her students have autism, Kay has a strong interest in autism research and awareness. She loves to spend time with her family, travel, and read in her free time. She can be contacted via e-mail at Kaysibkids@gmail.com*

7.
Happily Ever After?

Emily Marino

Throughout my dating life, my brother, Peter, has been in the habit of killing off my ex-boyfriends.

Some have gone down with the Titanic. Others were "exterminated" Dalek-style, a mysterious technique inspired by the android enemies of Peter's British sci-fi hero, *Dr. Who*.

"Hey Emily," he would say, days after a break-up, a mischievous gleam in his hazel eyes. "Look at this, your old boyfriend is history! Bye-bye, Sucker!" he would shout gleefully, clutching his pen in the awkward way he had learned as a child, cackling at his pad of paper. On the page, the Titanic would lie sinking, a tiny stick figure bobbing in the water beside it.

Peter is two years older than I and he has fragile X syndrome. Growing up outside of Boston, Peter always enjoyed writing and drawing. His carefully crafted sketches and stories often revealed—with startling understanding and humor—the perceptions, thoughts, and feelings that he could not always articulate.

Whenever I parted ways with a boyfriend, I knew that his death by Peter's hand was imminent. It was Peter's way of cutting ties, of getting even if he felt that I had been wronged, or of telling me that it was OK to move on.

From the time I began to date, in my teens, Peter was my "litmus test" of whether or not a guy was true boyfriend material. Was he nice to Peter? Nervous? Too nice, insincere?

Because we didn't have a name for what makes Peter different until he was much older, I could not prepare any of my prospective boyfriends by saying anything as straightforward as, "My brother has mental retardation." I might have said that Peter was "different," but this was always frustrating, uncomfortable, and seemingly unfair to Peter, the guy, and me.

Afraid of being rejected for all of the typical reasons known to adolescent girls, I was also aware, even then, that Peter and I were ultimately a two-for-one deal. I was not actively contemplating the day when our parents would pass on and I would be responsible to whatever extent for my brother. But on some level I knew that whoever had a future with me would have to accept that Peter would be part of it. On top of acne, braces, and one or two bad hairdos, this was a lot to worry about.

And so I did what many young women do for a variety of reasons: I dated guys who I knew, from the outset, would never disappoint me because they could never meet my expectations in the first place. I began dating The Wrong Guy.

My first boyfriend in high school—I'll call him The Rebel— seemed like the right guy at the time. He wore tie-dyed T-shirts and applied his considerable intelligence to finding ways to break rules without getting into trouble. Dating him was, for me, an act of safe rebellion. I was a good student and obedient daughter who believed that getting high grades and staying out of trouble would compensate for the problems that my brother had at school and home. Spending time with The Rebel, who so joyfully challenged the boundaries of adolescent life, provided me with an escape from my overachieving, perfection-seeking world.

Most importantly, he passed the "litmus test."

"S-s-stop!" Peter would shout through fits of laughter and The Rebel's playful headlock. Both were over six feet tall and their wrestling looked slightly ridiculous.

"Come on, Peter, show me how tough you are!" The Rebel would reply, losing his balance as Peter brought both of them to the ground.

I rolled my eyes at their childish behavior, but I loved that he treated Peter like the rest of his friends. Peter, whose disabilities are social as well as cognitive, did not have many friends his own age and he loved spending time with us. The Rebel was not afraid to talk to Peter and he was never condescending when he did. He enjoyed spending time with Peter, but he knew not to cross the fine line that I had drawn as a sibling who wanted her boyfriend to accept and love her brother without putting his needs first.

"Hey Pete, tonight I'm taking your sister out for dinner, but we're all going out next week, right?"

The Rebel and I broke up when I went away to college. I felt guilty that my brother was losing a friend in addition to losing me. When I left, a part of me felt that I was abandoning Peter and our parents. While I was making new friends and exploring career possibilities, Peter was stuck at home, socially isolated, and, although he had a job, anxious about his future. Unlike many of my friends' parents, ours were not able to enjoy a newly emptied nest.

This guilt stayed with me throughout my twenties, after I moved to New York City and continued to date The Wrong Guy. Peter remained at home with our parents and continued to work. Some of my boyfriends eventually made it into Peter's notebook. Some were great guys who simply weren't ready for the commitment that I was beginning to want but wasn't sure I deserved.

My favorite and most common dating mistake was The Fixer-Upper. This was the guy who was emotionally unavailable and unstable in his career, but who, with just a little bit of love and support, I was sure, would be a wonderful partner. By fixing these guys, I decided, we could all live happily ever after.

The most memorable ending to a relationship with a Fixer-Upper took place in a famously romantic Manhattan restaurant on Valentine's Day.

"So, you know that this is where they filmed that scene in *Moonstruck,* right?" the Fixer-Upper asked. We had met playing softball in a city league and had been dating since the summer. He was a charismatic, smart but unmotivated, part-time student who, despite not having a regular income, prided himself on hanging out at the trendiest restaurants and clubs.

"Um, yeah, I think I remember that," I lied. I have a terrible memory for movies, and have been known to be halfway through a film before realizing that I've seen it before.

"It was almost impossible to get this reservation on Valentine's Day, but I talked to some people because I wanted to do something special for you."

"Yes, well, thank you," I said, thinking that dinner for him was more about being able to tell people where we had eaten than it was about enjoying a romantic evening with me.

At the end of the meal, The Fixer-Upper surprised me not with a diamond ring or a dozen roses, but by revealing that he had no money and that, by the way, they only accepted cash.

It was then that I realized, with a flash of anger at myself, that I was wasting my time—wasting my life, really. Just as I would never be able to "fix" my brother, I was not going to transform anyone from an ambitionless drifter into Mr. Right.

And then a new fear hit me.

What if there *was* no Mr. Right? What if there wasn't a man out there who would love me and my family, with all of our quirks and imperfections? And even if he existed, did I really deserve him? Why should I be happy when Peter was alone and miserable at home? How could I ever get married, start a family, and abandon my parents and brother?

As I worried about never finding Mr. Right, many of my friends got married. How could they be so sure, I wondered, that they had found their partners for life?

I thought about all that our parents had endured with Peter over the years—endless medical testing, fights with school districts to ensure that he got the education to which he was entitled, constant vigilance and advocacy to make sure that he was not discriminated against at work. All of this had tested our parents' marriage, and although there were certainly stressful, dark moments, they remained committed to each other and to us, in good times and bad.

I did not wish these challenges upon any of my friends, but I wondered if I had a different idea of what matrimony was really about. And I felt angry and sad that I was unable to so easily share their belief in "happily ever after."

This was especially true when, one by one, my friends started to have children.

Since seeing a graphic documentary in middle school about the miracle of life (a brilliant way for schools to combat teen pregnancy), I have never been a fan of childbirth. Nine months of physical discomfort followed by several hours of excruciating pain just isn't my thing.

"But you forget the pain," my mother once said, after I had proclaimed that I was never having kids. "Because afterwards you have this little baby and it's all worth it."

That part scared me even more, especially the thought of having a baby with a developmental disability or delay. Because we had never known what Peter's disability was or where it came from, I worried about passing it on to my children.

Even if a doctor could tell me what my chances are of giving birth to a child with a disability, what would I do with that information? Would I trust it? How would I use it to decide whether or not to have a baby? Would I have a child if there was a thirty percent chance of a disability? Fifty percent? Seventy?

In sharing my fears with other women in their twenties and thirties who have siblings with developmental disabilities, I learned that I was not alone.

One friend whose brother has Asperger's syndrome said that she's afraid that she will disappoint her husband and in-laws and feel forever guilty if she doesn't give them "a perfect baby."

Another decided that, since she grew up taking care of her brother who has Down syndrome and will do so after their parents are gone, she did not want the added responsibility of children. She married a man who doesn't want kids, either.

A friend whose brother has autism adopted a baby girl. Another is pregnant with her first child and hoping for the best.

As for me, I still don't know about having kids.

But I finally realized that I deserve to be happy, and to share my life with someone—an equal partner—able to reciprocate all of the love and support that I was ready to give.

And then I found him.

Tom is wonderful for many reasons. He is intelligent, honest, and genuinely funny. He has a tremendous work ethic and loyal dedication to family and friends. He doesn't mind that I forget movies.

And of course he passed the "litmus test."

Peter loves spending time with Tom, and that Tom times his haircuts with our visits so that they can go to the barber together. Tom appreciates Peter's imagination and his gleeful cackle. He understands that one day I will have greater responsibility in ensuring Peter's well being, and he wants to be by my side.

When Tom and I got engaged, I called home and Peter answered the phone. He was the first to hear the news.

"Hey, Peter, isn't that great? We're going to be brothers-in-law!" Tom said before passing the phone back to me.

Peter's response made me realize that, in all the years that I had worried about "leaving" my brother, I hadn't understood that when I got married, he would gain something too.

"I am so happy for you, Emily," Peter said. "You know, Tom is the best one you have ever had. I'm glad that he is going to be part of our family."

"Thanks, Peter," I said. "So I guess I won't be seeing him in any of your stories?"

"Oh yes you will," he said. "He's going to be part of my adventures, and all of us will live happily ever after."

* * *

Emily Marino is the Senior Manager of Writing at YAI/National Institute for People with Disabilities, a New York City based not-for-profit organization which provides services to people of all ages with developmental disabilities and their families. She is a member of the Sibling Leadership Network, a national organization dedicated to connecting the siblings of individuals with developmental disabilities to one another and to providing them with the information, resources, and support to make a positive difference in their families' lives. Emily lives in Brooklyn, New York, with three cats and her "Mr. Right," Tom.

8.
The Mess We're In

Tara Kosieniak

My brother, Nicholas, is twenty-nine and lives with our parents, as he has for most of his life. Nick has cerebral palsy, muscular dystrophy, and severe intellectual disabilities, just to name a few. Nick is nonverbal and uses a wheelchair, but is still the happiest person you'll ever meet. When you visit with him, he is always smiling, laughing, and wants to hug and kiss you. His favorite times of the year are Christmas and his birthday because he loves opening presents.

Recently, the issue of planning for Nick's future has come into play because my parents are getting older and their health is not the greatest. The process of planning for the future for someone with special needs can be difficult, but my family has made it impossible. The problem is my father has turned it into something secretive and extremely painful to talk about. Due to his inaction and lack of communication, we are facing a crisis that has torn our family apart.

My mom and I have done everything in our power to avert this crisis, but my dad has refused to listen to our pleas. My mom felt the only thing she could do was file for a divorce. She did not want to do this, but felt it was the only way to make my father listen and force him to make some plans for the future. Since my father was served with divorce papers, I have hardly spoken with him. It's not because I don't want to communicate with him, but he won't answer my calls or e-mails. I somehow feel like he is blaming me for the divorce. Because things are so contentious, I am more uncertain of Nick's future than ever. Part of the problem is that my father won't tell us what he wants for Nick after he is gone.

Not a day goes by that I don't think about how my family has become such a mess. I wonder why my dad is being so stubborn, and wish we could talk about Nick's future openly, as a family. I don't understand why everything about Nick's care and future has to be such a secret with my father and wonder why my father won't talk to me anymore. All I ever wanted was to make sure Nick would be cared for in the days to come—which is the primary reason I chose a career working with people who have disabilities.

I completed my graduate and undergraduate work in Human Services and Psychology and have worked with people with developmental disabilities for the past seventeen years. I chose this work because I wanted to know everything there was to know about the services and options for people like my brother. I knew one day I would have to oversee things for Nick and his care. This was my way of contributing to the care of my brother because I knew I would never be able to care for him physically.

Maybe my father thinks that Nicholas will just live with me after they pass. Although I would like that to happen, it would be impossible for many reasons. First, I don't have the financial resources needed to devote to his care. Second, I don't have a house that is equipped for his special needs. Third and most importantly, I cannot physically take care of Nicholas. I too have a disability; it's called Charot-Marie-Tooth. It is a type of muscular dystrophy that affects my strength, coordination, and circulation. My mother has this as well and I have seen first-hand how her health and well-being have deteriorated over the years because of it, complicated by physical demands of my brother. Her health is so bad now that she can barely care for herself anymore.

A year has gone by since my mother filed for divorce. My mother and father still live in the same household but hardly speak to each other. The only communication between them has to do with Nick's daily care. As a result of the tension caused by the divorce proceedings, my husband and I no longer visit—something we did every Sunday and on most holidays. We didn't want to stop, but we don't feel welcome any longer. This has made me very sad because I enjoyed visiting my family and seeing my brother.

As a result of the divorce proceedings, my father finally completed a will and set up a special needs trust. However, the special needs trust is written incorrectly. My mother and I had a lawyer review it—and as it is written, it could jeopardize Nick's care. My father wrote me out of his will and the special needs trust. He now has my uncle as the beneficiary and my cousin as the executor of the trust.

Because he won't talk to me, I don't know or understand why he did this. I can only speculate that he thinks my mother and I are after his money. This is the saddest thing of all because if it is true, it tells me that he's never really known me or how much I care for my brother and my family. It makes me believe that he doesn't understand that I devoted my life to my career because of my love for my brother. I want Nick to have the best that life has to offer.

I have not given up all hope. I continue to believe that my father will someday understand why my mom and I have tried so hard to get him to talk about Nick's future. We hope that my father will open up and share his hopes and dreams for Nick. For now all I can do is pray that my father will do the right thing and that all is well in the end.

I hope parents who read this understand that planning for the future of a child with a disability is extremely important. It is more than just having a will and the right special needs trust. It's about building the person's support network and making sure everyone in that network knows the hopes and dreams you have for your child. Siblings are part of that support network. Parents need to include siblings in the future planning process because they are the ones who are going to carry out the plans and oversee the sibling's future.

I also hope that service providers encourage parents to include siblings in the future planning process. As a service provider, I've always encouraged parents to plan for the future of their child with special needs and to involve brothers and sisters in the process. I have had success teaching and helping other families complete this process—ironically, more success than I have had with my own family.

* * *

Tara Kosieniak has worked with people with disabilities for seventeen years, starting at age sixteen, when she provided respite to children and adults with developmental disabilities. After college, she became a QMRP (Qualified Mental Retardation Professional) for Community Support Services in Brookfield, Illinois, where she started offering Sibshops in 2000. Tara has been an active member of SibNet listserv since 1997 and has been a moderator for SibKids since 2002. In 2004, she started the listserv AdultSibsNet, modeled after SibNet but for adult siblings in Illinois. Tara co-founded Family Sibday for families whose children attend Sibshops. Additionally, Tara serves on the Sibling Support Project's Advisory Committee and the Sibling Leadership Network. Most recently, she has worked with other sibs in Illinois to create the nonprofit SIBS (Supporting Illinois Brothers and Sisters).

9.
Don't Apologize for Being a Brother

Zach Rossetti

As soon as the door closed and we heard Mom's car drive away, Todd and I looked at each other and began to laugh.

The day had started out like many others. As the oldest of six children, I was often asked to stay home with some combination of younger siblings while Mom ran errands. Very quickly, however, the day took an unexpected turn. For one thing, only Todd and I were home, rare in a family with six children. For another, it was mid-winter in New Hampshire and it had snowed the day before. Drifts of snow adorning the hill beyond our backyard beckoned us as in a wintry, Granite State version of the film *Field of Dreams:* "If you sled it," it seemed to say, "you will laugh." Like the character Ray Kinsella played by Kevin Costner, we could not ignore the voice.

I was seventeen years old and a junior in high school at the time. Todd was ten and in the third grade. Despite growing up in New Hampshire, we had never gone sledding together. I helped him put on his coat, grabbed the plastic sled, and lifted him out of his wheelchair. Todd laughs with his whole body. I consider it one of the many bonuses of his cerebral palsy since it is virtually impossible not to join him in his glee. However, his body erupted into laughter as soon as we stepped outside, and I almost dropped him. In order to prevent that mishap and because it was difficult trudging through the deep snow while holding him, I laid Todd down in the sled and pulled him up to the top of the hill.

As I joined my brother on the sled, thinking, "I can't believe we haven't done this before," Todd looked up at me with anticipation in his eyes. "Ready?!" I asked. Todd laughed his approval and I pushed off. The slow start gave way to rapid acceleration.

For a moment, our ride was perfect. Within seconds, though, we hit a bump and spun in midair. Todd landed face down in the snow and I landed on top of him. I rolled off quickly, and could see his shoulders heaving. I rolled him over and noticed the blood on his lip. Not a good sign. He was still heaving, but there were no tears. He was laughing—and continued to laugh the entire way home. Even though I was terrified, I laughed as well. How would I explain this one?

By the time we were back inside, a small lump had formed above Todd's right eye. I turned on the television for Todd, then held some ice cubes in a wet washcloth on his brow while I tried to figure out what to tell Mom. Before long, her van pulled up. Before she could greet us, I blurted out that we had gone sledding and crashed and Todd hurt his lip and eye. "I'm sorry." I said. "I didn't mean to."

Silence.

She turned to Todd and asked, "Did you go sledding with Zach?" Todd nearly leapt out of his wheelchair, straightening with excitement and his signature body laugh, his right arm waving in the air.

"Nice eye," she said.

She turned back to me and I expected the worst. "Don't ever be sorry for being a brother." With that she started to walk away, but turned back after a second's pause. "Just don't fall next time."

The thing is, I had already internalized this message. Todd's disability was never a tragedy in my eyes. Todd was always just Todd. He has a remarkable laugh, loves the Red Sox, loves chocolate cake even more, wants to be a poet, and takes a little longer to go places because he needs help getting dressed and it takes a few minutes to load his wheelchair into the accessible van. Todd's visible sledding injuries challenged this understanding for me. My mother's words were a powerful reminder. Todd is my brother.

Seventeen years later I still carry her words closely in all that I do. While I occasionally wish that Todd could have played pond hockey with us and at times I get frustrated with the necessity and monotony of his daily personal care (and experience guilt afterwards for feeling that way), I love and accept Todd as he is—just as I love and accept my other brothers and sisters for who they are. This is entirely due to the tireless efforts of our mother and the values she quietly instilled in us.

Whenever there was a sports game, a dance recital, a related practice or rehearsal (and there were many of them with six of us!), or any other family outing, there was never any question that Todd would be with us. She rounded us up, hollered at us, did whatever worked to get us ready to leave earlier so we could have time to get Todd into his wheelchair and strapped into the van. She always spoke to Todd as if he understood what she was saying. She called us out if we changed the television channel when he was watching something. When she asked us to feed him or to help her get him in bed, we did. The strength of her absolute expectation that Todd would go to school and live as we all did permeated our household. She never explained his disability, why we needed to help, or that she knew it might be difficult for us. It was not that she did not think about these things constantly, because she did. It was simply her conviction that Todd was, well, Todd. He was not deficient or special, a burden or a blessing. He was who he was, and the things that needed to be done were done.

I consider it a tragedy that most of Todd's classmates and teachers over the years missed out on the privilege of getting to know him as we do. Spending time with him is my favorite thing to do in the world. He has so much to offer—he is outgoing and smart and funny. He is playful and sarcastic and interesting. He is unique. And yet, very few people know this.

Granted, getting to know Todd can be a bit challenging because Todd does not speak. A potential friend would need an accessible vehicle (or be trusted by our mother to drive the accessible van) since he gets around in a wheelchair. He also tends to fatigue and overheat easily, so late night and summer excursions can be difficult. But these issues seem insignificant relative to the rewards of knowing him. As it is for too many other adults with disabilities, Todd's biggest problem is loneliness.

When we are walking downtown or watching our youngest brother's hockey games, kids and adults always come over to say hi. Todd will reach out to most anyone with his right hand (the one movement he can control), and always shakes hands. Since he is usually smiling or laughing, the many people who know him seem to enjoy interacting with him. I used to smile when this happened, thinking that he had made friends. However, as the years passed, the phone never rang for Todd and he only left the house with our family. I wondered, "How can someone who is so cool and seems so popular never get invited to go out with friends after school and on the weekends?"

Over time, I began to realize that there was less to these social interactions than I had envisioned. The interactions were initiated, controlled, and ended by others—and they were relatively transient. Adults often exaggerated their greetings, speaking in a louder, baby-ing voice and typically following the same paternal script. Greetings by peers were made in passing, the interactions joyous and legitimate but also awkward and brief as the kids would continue moving on to hang out with their "real" friends. Because Todd's immediate response resulted in instant gratification, the goal seemed always to be to shake his hand and make him laugh. These exaggerated or brief interactions were surface exchanges at best, rarely extending beyond the walls of the school and the timeframe of school activities. Todd was popular, but he was lonely, too.

Todd's ongoing social isolation pains me the most—more than the occasional stare, the low expectations, and staff turnover in adult developmental disabilities services, or even the ongoing inaccessibil-ity of many of our favorite restaurants and bars. I was born to be a teacher, and I chose special education largely because of my experi-ences growing up with Todd. Still, I cannot shake the feeling that

I should be doing more for him. But what? We have held person-centered planning meetings, we try to take advantage of any and all social opportunities in the community, and we continue to search for ways to support him to develop social connections.

Ironically, being in the field of special education makes this even more difficult. I should be able to help figure out how to increase Todd's community involvement. I have made a career out of developing individualized academic and social supports, and I champion inclusive schools and communities. Yet, I can't find a way to make this happen for Todd. I never felt the embarrassment, resentment, anger, or neglect that is often described in the research on sibling experiences. But I ache with frustration and guilt at not being able to help solve the problem of Todd's inactivity and social isolation. At times, it seems insurmountable. It makes me wonder how difficult it must be for other families and siblings who do not have a background in special education and inclusion to deal with similar issues.

Currently, our family's biggest challenge continues to be supporting Todd so he can live on his own, find meaningful employment, and develop some friendships and social connections with his peers. It is frightening and frustrating that almost six years have passed since his high school graduation—when we were all so optimistic for his future—and now he spends most of his days sitting in front of the television at our mother's house. He never misses a Red Sox game, but he is missing out on life. So much time and effort went into ensuring that he experienced the most effective and most inclusive schooling possible. But the following years have felt like a purgatory in which the hope of achieving his goals diminishes daily.

I want to agree with our mother. Todd is just Todd. But if these last six years have taught me anything, it is that things do not work out just because you want them to or think they should. The elusive goal is to help Todd get beyond surface level interactions and develop meaningful relationships and experiences. I just keep thinking, Todd needs fewer high fives and more opportunities for sledding.

* * *

Zachary Rossetti *is an assistant professor in the Elementary Special Education program at Providence College. He recently finished his Ph.D. in Special Education from Syracuse University. His doctoral dissertation,* Learning to Connect: Developmental Disability and Friendship in High School, *is a qualitative study of three groups of high school students with and without developmental disabilities who are friends. Zach co-produced and co-directed (with Douglas Biklen) the documentary short* My Classic Life as an Artist: A Portrait of Larry Bissonnette *(2005). The film won Best Short at the 16th annual Vermont International Film Festival (2005) and the 2005 TASH Image Award. Zach co-authored (with Carol Tashie and Susan Shapiro-Barnard)* Seeing the Charade: What We Need to Do and Undo to Make Friendships Happen *(2006). Zach was born and raised in New Hampshire and currently resides in Brookline, MA.*

10.
Aunty Danni

Yona Lunsky

One evening before bed, my four-year-old son, Gabriel, asked, "Why does Aunty Danni call me Gabi-ol? I hate when she calls me that."

"Well," I said, "I think sometimes she forgets how to say your name properly. And she has a hard time pronouncing *r's.*" Then I needed to add, "She doesn't mean to do that. Aunty Danni loves you very much, you know."

"Yeah, I know, Mom. . . ." Gabriel responded in an understanding way. Then he added "Hey! There are some kids in my kindergarten who also can't say their *r's* either!"

Sometimes my boys ask me benign questions like that about my sister. Other times, the questions are a bit more challenging: *Why does Aunty Danni hug so tight? Why does she have staff? When will she learn to drive? How come she doesn't know how to read very well?*

Danni is the third of four children and I am the youngest. Growing up, we were very close. We shared a bedroom for almost fifteen years. When her siblings moved away, Danni also moved out—to a group home. But when we all became attached, she was left single. Having us get married was hard for Danni. It meant less exclusive time with us and she began to ask questions about when she would get married.

During my first two years of marriage, Danni and I did things together, and sometimes we included my husband in our plans. Danni would sleep over at our apartment in the guest room, and we'd go shopping, out to dinner, or to see a movie.

Then I got pregnant. Danni was as excited about this as I was and told everyone she knew. She didn't understand when the baby would be born (she'd tell people it was happening tomorrow); she couldn't understand how it made me feel (tired); and she certainly didn't know the impact a baby would have on our relationship—but then, neither did I.

Danni, my brother, and my other sister are my oldest son Avi's godparents. She was honored to be a godparent, but being around him as a baby was hard. We wouldn't let her hold the baby unless she was sitting down, even though other people could carry the baby standing up. She didn't realize that Avi couldn't understand what she was saying to him. She would say "hello" and wave her hand close to his face, and sometimes asked him a question or two. She would wait for the reply, and my husband and I would need to remind her that he couldn't speak yet. As he got a bit older, she wanted to hug him too often or too tightly and lift him off the floor, which made us nervous. We wanted her around, but it was difficult, and soon she stopped sleeping over. Between her, the baby, and our cat, no one could get any sleep.

I am sure that Danni sensed my anxiety, which only contributed to her anxiety. I know that Danni must have missed the old times when it was just the two of us. Because there was just one baby, we eventually discovered ways to do things so it still felt like just two of us. We would put Avi in the stroller and shop for groceries or take him out with us for dinner. And although we could no longer go to the movies, we could still watch a movie together at home. We made the adjustments and it wasn't that different.

As Avi grew older, some things got simpler. I was less sleep-deprived and I could be away from him for longer periods, which meant that sometimes Danni and I could spend time alone together again. But to Danni, toddlers were as frustrating as babies. Danni has a short attention span. She would sit down and very happily read a storybook or listen to music with Avi but then unexpectedly she would be ready to move on. Sometimes, she'd lose interest and drop the toy or book and walk away. Other times, she would grab the item from Avi before walking away.

On one occasion, she told one of her nephews that she was going to Florida. He said, as two-year-olds like to do, "No!" Perhaps she did not understand that this little boy did not have the power to restrict her from going to Florida or maybe she was just reacting to his emotion, but she became very upset, yelling at our nephew and crying because she was told she could not go to Florida. I learned then that Danni can't differentiate content from the speaker. She has no way of reasoning that the speaker is not reliable.

No doubt these experiences were frustrating and difficult for Aunty Danni, but they were also hard for me as the mother. Danni could not play with my son or her other nieces and nephews unsupervised. Danni did not have permission to do things with babies and toddlers that other grown-ups had. And Danni could no longer have as much attention from me.

As I had more children, I hoped Danni's experience with Avi, my eldest, would make things easier, but it didn't. In fact, they seemed to get harder. When my first son was born, we could all take turns being with the baby and being with Danni. However, with two and then three small children around, there were fewer grown-ups to give Danni exclusive attention. These days, I can rarely give anyone exclusive attention, Danni included. With more children, family dinners have become louder and less predictable, and everything is more chaotic.

Each year, our family celebrates Chanukah, which falls around Danni's birthday. Before there were nine nieces and nephews, Chanukah meant a lot of presents for Danni. She opened each one with sheer delight and loved being showered with attention. Now there are presents for the nieces and nephews. Danni gets presents too, but the frenzied energy in the air from lots of children giddy with their gifts is overwhelming and if Danni's needs are forgotten, she ends up feeling frustrated.

It has been a few years now since Danni has slept over, largely because it has been a few years since my house has been quiet at night. Someone is always waking up and that kind of noise is not OK for Danni. I also worry that Danni will wake up my kids with the noise she sometimes makes.

So I have Danni come over for dinner instead. My kids love to go with me to get her from her group home. We pick up some barbequed chicken, bring it home, and have dinner together. Afterwards, we listen to favorite CDs from Danni's and my childhood and my kids love to watch us sing and dance. We clean the kitchen and have dessert, and soon Danni is asking when she can go home. These evenings require organization and coordination and I have to make sure my husband is home as an extra pair of hands. They don't last long but we try to make sure they end well.

When dinner isn't possible, my kids and I sometimes visit Danni and walk to the park. She gets bored of the swings and slides pretty quickly, but she has a few moments where she can be the proud aunt, swinging her nephew or chasing him around a tree. Again, we try to end these brief visits on a good note.

Unfortunately, the visits don't always go so well. Sometimes Danni gets frustrated being with my boys and says "you're bugging me" or "stop staring at me." At first, my kids didn't know what to do with Danni's comments, particularly if she yelled at them with a threatening voice. It took them a while to understand that trying to explain that they weren't staring at her would not ease her agitation. It took them even longer not to take her anger personally. Now they know that these outbursts are something Danni does sometimes and that the best response is to ignore her. It's her way of saying she needs some quiet or some space.

Although we don't do them as frequently as we used to, Danni and I still try to do special activities together, just the two of us. Because they are so rare, I savor these experiences. For Danni's thirty-ninth birthday, she came over for dinner with my family, and then the two of us went out together to see a play and sat third row center.

It was fantastic. It was a musical that we both love, and the two of us sang in the theater and all the way home.

In less than twelve years, Danni has gone from being the center of attention to having nine nieces and nephews. She can't explain how all of this has affected her, but I can talk about how it has affected me. Although I tell myself that I am doing my best and that being hard on myself won't help, there are days when I feel very guilty about my decreased day-to-day involvement with my sister. At those times, I remind myself that my relationship with Danni is lifelong. I have had times in my life that she was my first priority. I will have time again in the future that I can devote more time to her. But not now. My kids need me, and I must be careful because if I burn out now, it won't be good for anyone.

There are other days when I feel very proud and blessed—proud of Danni and proud of my boys. She delights in seeing them and they love being warmly greeted by her. They are interested in her stories of her roommates and the people she works with, and she responds enthusiastically to their stories, even if she doesn't understand them. Even my two-year-old loves to talk with his Aunty Danni on the phone. She never tires of him saying the same things to her over and over. If I can make sure that the times we spend together are good, then Danni's future will involve not only me but also my children. We all have so much we can learn from each other.

* * *

Yona Lunsky is a clinical psychologist in Toronto. She leads a research program in Dual Diagnosis (developmental disabilities and mental health concerns) at the Centre for Addiction and Mental Health, linked to the Department of Psychiatry at the University of Toronto. Yona publishes extensively on issues related to the health and well-being of adults with developmental disabilities, but this is her first personal essay. Her main hobby right now is her family. All family members (including her sister) love music and hanging out. In rare quiet moments, Yona is learning to knit.

11.
Breathe In, Relax

Dirk Stanley

"I'll get it, Daddy!" the boy shouted repeatedly, as he ran across the yard, almost tripping over his oversized clown shoes. His dad, Laughing Larry the Clown (yes, names have been changed to protect the innocent), had been hired by my brother's group home as a welcome-to-the-neighborhood gesture for my brother. My parents were apprehensive about my brother moving from the quiet, clean air of the Hudson River Valley in upstate New York, down to this more metropolitan group home, but when the administration threw a party to welcome him to the group home, it seemed like a genuine and heartwarming gesture.

Laughing Larry didn't seem to totally understand what he was getting into. What probably started as "You're going to be entertaining some kids with special needs!" turned out to be something very different. For some people, I suppose the term "special needs" conjures up images of demure kids in wheelchairs—the children typically seen in made-for-TV movies, or standing quietly next to Jerry Lewis while he asks for donations in his yearly telethon. But most people don't realize how far the term "special needs" can go, or what it can look like in real life.

Laughing Larry unfortunately had to learn the hard way. He brought his son, aged about twelve, who also wore clown makeup and shoes while he proudly joined his father in entertaining clients. Larry and son showed up at my brother's group home with their "bag of tricks," a big red satchel out of which Larry pulled various balloons, magic wands, hats, and very well-intentioned tricks. The only problem was my brother and his fellow group home residents didn't quite get the joke.

Now, the following may be embellished somewhat, and time has faded my memory of the exact details, but here's what I remember about Larry's education regarding the word "special needs," especially when applied to kids in this particular group home.

First, the "kids" turned out to be adults in their thirties. Not little cherubic-faced, gleamy-eyed children, but adults with facial stubble and faint body odor and outdated clothes from the eighties. So when Larry blew up balloons, and formed them into delicate animals, and gave them out to my brother's fellow residents, he didn't get the youthful, appreciative, beaming smiles of a child's face. Instead, he watched several of the adults put his carefully crafted balloon animals in their mouths, at which point they were chewed and *popped,* the balloons deflating in a symbolic gesture to Larry's comedic ego.

Larry then gave my brother a magic wand and asked him to tap on the hat from which Larry planned to extract a small animal. Unfortunately, my brother decided instead to chew on Larry's magic wand, causing the now-upset Larry to frantically try to wrestle his wand out of my brother's mouth, while my brother continued chewing on it, smiling back at him.

And during his final trick, one of my brother's housemates sneaked behind Larry and opened his satchel. Apparently the aborted animal-in-the-hat-trick involved a live dove, because suddenly Larry's dove fluttered across the yard, up into a tree branch high up above. Larry's son chased after it, almost tripping over his oversized clown shoes. I sat there, helpless but giggling, watching as a depressed frown sneaked out from beneath Larry's clown-makeup smile, contradicting his bright aura. And no, as far as I know, they never got the dove back.

Larry and son left the party a little early. I tried to thank him for his efforts, but he drove off before I could reach him.

And so goes the life of a sibling of a person with a severe disability. Your life is filled with moments that are simultaneously hysterical and heartbreaking. Groucho Marx himself couldn't have written comedy like this, nor would he have wanted to. Through an endless stream of these moments, you realize that your life is going to be a little different. If nothing else, you look at birthday clowns in a whole new way.

But more importantly, you realize that there are people who *really* understand—and then there is everyone else. It's almost like being in the military. You go through boot camp and learn a whole new way of seeing the world. It's very polarizing and the world gets divided in two groups: People who are living it, and civilians. You can't really blame civilians for not understanding; after all, they didn't go through boot camp like you did. But sometimes you wish they understood what you're living with. And you wish you had a choice of whether or not to enlist in this particular army.

Then you have to decide about what you'll do with this new education—an education you sometimes wish you didn't have. Some people will dwell on the sorrow, the tragedy, the heartbreak, and the misfortune of watching a group of adults with disabilities send a clown and his son home with tears in their eyes. And myself, I suppose, I've decided to let it guide me toward making the best of a bad situation. After all, how can you not laugh?

It wasn't always like that. There were years where our family struggled with grasping the realities of my brother's disability. We learned we weren't going to have quiet dinners, politely chatting about politics or celebrities. Instead, our nightly dinners would be an emotional balancing act where we'd "try to act normal" while keeping an eye out for my brother, who would grab food from our plates with his lightening-fast hands. We didn't go to shopping malls to leisurely shop for clothes or get a snack at McDonald's. Instead, we tried to "act normal" by holding my brother's hands tightly and praying he wouldn't grab the food of a passerby. (There's nothing worse than having a mother yell at you because your brother stole her kid's ice cream.) And my parents had to learn that one of their sons wasn't going to graduate from college, let alone high school, let alone trade school, let alone grade school. One of their two children was going to be in a group home for the rest of his life, and small victories in behavior would be hard won.

But eventually, you have two choices: Either let the situation ruin you and your whole family, or find some way to let it make you stronger. I suppose our family figured out, after many years of struggle, how to do the latter.

Once you make the decision to take a bad situation and turn it around, and to smile at life, it can have some pretty profound effects. I used what I learned to help care for people, first for people with disabilities in college, and later at medical school, where I eventually became a doctor.

I think I'm a pretty good doctor, but there are lots of good doctors who will work long hours trying hard to help their patients. But if you ask people who work with me about *how* I'm different from a lot of good doctors, most will tell you about my handwriting.

Remember, doctors aren't known for legible handwriting, and many doctors' notes require lots of squinting to decipher the hieroglyphics entered into a medical chart. And yet, I work hard to make sure every word of my notes is legible. So why do I obsess about this?

The answer has everything to do with my brother. Having grown up with someone with whom I've never been able to have a conversation (he's nonverbal), I look at communication in a very different way. I know, on a deep, personal level, how tragic it is to be unable to communicate an idea with someone you love. Siblings grow up with this frustration. And I'm not just paying lip service to the idea of "communication is good." My heart *bleeds* when I think about the many barriers there are to communication, from age barriers, to time barriers, to cultural barriers, to language barriers, and to disability barriers, to educational barriers.

So when I write my notes, the *last* thing I want is for someone not to understand me because they can't read my handwriting.

Communication is tough enough as it is. What a beautiful gift we have, the ability to speak to each other, in the same language, sharing ideas, letting others know what we're thinking and finding out what they're thinking. Without the gift of communication, I imagine I would be like a heartbroken Ebenezer Scrooge, being shown around by the Ghost of Christmas Past, shouting at the people he loved, only to see they can't hear his thoughts. What a tragic feeling that must be. I often wonder if my brother feels the same way.

But most of us have the remarkable gift of communication. We're able to share ideas. We speak and hear words, we see body language, and we read actions. My experiences with my brother make me cherish this gift. Sometimes I daydream about how it must have felt to read the first telegram delivered by the Pony Express, or to hear the first words spoken by Alexander Graham Bell, or to see the first sign language developed by Gallaudet, or to interpret Marconi's first wireless telegram from across the Atlantic, or to see the first e-mail sent over the Internet. All of these are significant efforts—just to find out what someone else is thinking—and beautiful demonstrations of communication.

And then I think about tragedies that arise from a lack of communication: the Titanic's crew helplessly wiring for rescue boats; Kitty Genovese screaming for the help that never came; Hurricane Katrina survivors waiting patiently for help to arrive; stroke victims suddenly unable to tell their families they love them. All are heartbreaks of absent or missed communication. After all, isn't living all about communication?

So given my lifetime of frustration at not being able to talk with someone close to me, I make the extra effort to make sure other people can understand me. When I talk to my patients, I take time to make sure they really understand why they're in the hospital and what our treatment plan is. And I try to apply the same rules to my own life and relationships, not wanting a day to slip by without letting someone know how I feel and finding out what they're feeling. I suppose it's interesting to consider that maybe my brother *does* communicate with me, in his own way. After all, these are the lessons he's taught us, without ever saying a word.

Here's my only advice to siblings and civilians alike when confronted with someone with a severe disability: Smile, don't sweat the
small stuff, try your best, communicate the best that you can, and
don't try too hard to be "normal." You'll ruin yourself in the process.
Just take a deep breath, and you'll see life in a whole new way that's really not all bad, if you can learn to open your eyes and appreciate it.

* * *

*Robert "Dirk" Stanley, a native of Hartsdale, New York, is the older
brother of Marc, who has autism, and the son of Robert and Doris
Stanley of Armonk, New York, who continue to advocate for Marc and
other people with autism. Dirk spent many years working with people
with disabilities in various capacities before going to medical school. He
now lives in Northampton, Massachusetts, where he practices general
medicine and helps people with disabilities with their medical issues.
Dirk and his wife, Leah, recently welcomed their first son, Thomas.*

12.
A Letter to my Brother

Nina C.

Dear Ben,

I've decided to write you a letter you will never read. I'm going to say all the things I would say if you didn't have a disability, if you lived in your own apartment and had your privacy, and if I didn't fear that anything I sent to you would be opened and read and interpreted and possibly censored or destroyed by our parents before it reached you.

Of course, if you had your own place and didn't have a disability, I wouldn't need to write this letter. But let's pretend for the sake of this letter that you could read this and that you could understand it. Just take a magic pill for the next few minutes while we have this discussion.

Our parents didn't quite know how to explain to us the fact that you are a little bit different from other people. They decided to tell you that you were perfectly fine, and that you were a good boy— that much was true. But they did not tell you that you were born with Down syndrome and that you will never be able to do some of the things you want to do—at least, not without a lot of support from other people. Our parents didn't have the heart to tell me that I would never, ever be able to make you like the brothers other kids have—brothers who grow up and become fully independent. They repeated cheerfully, "Oh he's exactly like other boys; he just needs more time to learn things." While I have come to realize this is not true, it looks like you still believe that.

It must be incredibly frustrating to be thirty-six years old, still living at home with our parents, with a curfew of 9:00 p.m., no driver's license, no socializing with anyone at work, no private phone calls, and no contact with your girlfriend unless our parents approve. If you're just like everyone else, then why are you being treated so differently? This is something you and I have never discussed, because I am afraid it would upset our parents, and they're the ones who have to live with you and take care of you every day.

So let me tell you something. You will probably never have a regular job like me, at least not without a job coach and many years of training. You will never fulfill your dream of graduating from law school, because your brain does not process information quickly and cannot handle complicated calculations. You know when you have trouble calculating the tip to leave in a restaurant? When you try and try and just can't get the answer right, and finally fling down a handful of bills without counting them? Trying to learn about the law would feel like that all the time—it would be very hard and frustrating for you, and when you came to the exams you would not be able to finish them in time. Let's face it: you are not going to be a lawyer like my friend L., who is your role model. You can do many other exciting things, but you won't get to practice law.

Let me tell you something else. You might get married, I suppose, but you probably won't be able to take care of children on your own. I strongly recommend that you do *not* have children (or get involved with a woman who has children), because I am not willing to help you look after them. In fact, I would be extremely angry with you if you had a child, because that would just create added responsibilities for me, more responsibility that I had not chosen, and that has been the story of my life so far.

Just to be clear, I'm not mad at you because you were born different—I love you just the way you are, with all your strengths and weaknesses. Every time I come back to visit you, I am astonished at your capacity to find humor in everyday situations and to be kind and generous to people who are having a hard time. I see that you are living your life with grace and patience despite all the limitations that frustrate you, and that you constantly reach out to others to form and reaffirm friendships. I admire your ability to be completely focused on the pleasures of a good meal or a simple card game, and to take sheer delight in sitting next to people you love. You create quirky paintings and sculptures that bring to life your imaginary world, and you sometimes make up your own words to songs everyone knows. Whenever I am feeling uncertain of my place in the world, your warm hug lets me know that being your sister—being myself—is enough.

But I do feel sad that at age thirty-seven, I haven't yet had the courage to start my own family because I've been so worried about plans for your long-term care. It has taken a long time to get our parents to agree to name me your alternate legal guardian and to get our parents to finally write their wills in a way that makes it possible for me to take care of you when they're gone. You haven't been a part of all this, but that's why we had all those meetings that you weren't allowed to attend. Sorry, Ben. I would have liked you to be part of the discussion, but our parents absolutely refused to discuss your future with me while you were present. That's why I have spent the last two years e-mailing service providers, trying to get supports set up for you, doing research on guardianship and trusteeship and wills and trust funds until my head was spinning. I've done a lot for you, Ben, and I think it's time for me to start living my own life for a change.

So here's my game plan. As I see it, your options are limited, but they are options that can give you a pretty good life. Your life right now is good. You live at home with our parents, who cook healthy Asian food, allow you to watch professional wrestling once a week, and drive you to enriching programs like the gym for people with disabilities, the art center, and the choir. You get to travel to the West Coast to visit your friend S., occasionally to New York to visit me, and make occasional field trips with the choir, or to the Rocky

Mountains with Mom. Papa takes you grocery shopping every Saturday. You are well known and beloved to the farmer's market regulars—the cheese lady knows your name and sets aside your favorite cheeses for you. In Chinatown, I've seen you interacting with the lady who sells tofu, who taught you a few words of Cantonese.

You take violin lessons with Mom and get to hang out with her students at recitals and after lessons. Some of her former students come by to visit you. We're hoping that K. and N. may soon become certified as personal supports for you, so that they can be paid to spend time taking you out shopping for fashionable clothes or attending sporting events—anything you want to do. Eight hours a week would give you a chance to do many things that other adults in their thirties do.

What more could you want? I know, you've told me repeatedly that you want to live independently, away from our parents. Certainly this will become necessary at some point, when our parents die. Here's one scenario: you could stay in our hometown, and my husband and I could find you a group home there. Somewhere with roommates who share some of your interests, not like X., whom you've said you don't like, because he roots for the hockey team you hate. I understand why you don't want to live with him, and I won't make you live in that apartment.

If you stay in our hometown, you could maintain your existing circle of friends, keep going to the art studio, singing in the choir—your whole routine would be the same as before. This would mean that my husband and I would have to spend time and money flying back and forth—coming to visit you frequently, well, maybe twice a year. I could come for a week at Christmas and a week in July for your birthday maybe. We'd talk on the phone once a week, pretty much like now. Every few years, I would attend your personal planning meeting and consult with your caregivers. Would that be enough for you? I don't know.

Another option would be for you to wait until our parents die, then move to New York to be closer to my husband and me. I don't know how long this would take or how complicated it would be. You might have to stay in Canada for a while, until we figure out the immigration details and the group home placement. Since I know someone at the local agency, I would be able to get information about services for you, and there are many group homes in New York, but there is also a waiting list, and who knows how old you would be at that point.

If we did this, you would have a whole new life—you'd have to make new friends, you would have new roommates, and you would have to learn a lot of new things. I could come and visit you more often, and you could come to visit me and my husband, staying overnight in our apartment for weekends once in a while. If you had health emergencies I would be nearby to look after you. Now that I think about it, I guess I would prefer it this way. You could be part of my life, meet my friends, and I would get to know your caregivers and your friends as well.

What do you say, Ben? How I wish we could actually have this conversation. It's hard trying to predict what you would want, and not being able to ask you directly. In the meantime, I suppose we'll have to keep on pretending that our parents will outlive you so that you'll never get a chance to live independently. That's the official story at home, anyway.

Your loving sister,
Nina

   * * *

Nina C. *is a writer, professor, and musician living in New York City. She can be reached at NinaCnyc@gmail.com.*

13.
Why I Am an "Uninvolved Sibling"

Anonymous

You are five. Or six—memory blurs to protect you. You are in your yellow-flowered pajamas even though the summer light still hangs heavy over the split-level suburban rooftops. Your mother ordered you into them early, when the unspoken tension always in the air grew taut as monofilament stretched across a staircase.

It's hard to run up the carpeted stairs in slipper-soled pajamas, but you have to. Behind you is the nightmare you live with. He is fifteen, maybe sixteen, heavy and long-armed and long-legged and reaching out to grab your pajama collar. It rips, but he trips on the stair and loses his grip. He roars in anger. You stumble upstairs, crying for your mother or father. They aren't there.

"Mustn't hit the girls. It's bad to hit the girls. Bad to hit the girls. Mustn't hit my sister." The voice behind you, thick and monotone and echolalic, coming ever closer, breath panting almost in your ear. Sweaty fingers hard and bruising on your narrow shoulder. You scream and twist away, sobbing even though you know it only feeds his rage. This is what he

wants, what in his broken mind will make up for everything he lost years before you were even conceived—your fear, your sobs, your blood.

He wants to kill you. You know that. Your parents refuse to recognize that.

The stairs are very short, but you are five, or six, and your legs don't move as fast as your terror. Somehow you make it to the top and run down the hall to your room, his footsteps lumbering behind. You've learned to slam the door and turn the little locking lever very quickly while he fumbles for the doorknob. This enrages him even more—you are smaller and weaker but you can think faster than he ever will—and the door shudders as he pounds on it.

You know what to do. You've done it twice this week already. You crawl under the pink-comfortered bed, dust stinging your nostrils, and shimmy back on your stomach until your slippered feet touch the wall. Fur brushes your leg: seal-colored with dark points, blue eyes wide with fear and hatred. The cat knows what to do too. His kicking her started the familiar drama. First the cat, then you. That's the way it always happens.

Now is the time to go silent. No crying allowed, not even for five- or six-year-old girls. You peek through the tiny gap where the comforter brushes the hardwood floor. Through it you can see the door shiver in its frame, almost as hard as you are shivering now. The cat's fur puffs up like a dandelion, but she stays silent too.

Then your father, loud and angry: "That's enough! Leave that door alone! Leave your sister alone!" The words are parroted back with glee. More shouting, your father cursing, your mother almost inaudible in the background, then the familiar thumps and groans of scuffling as your father—you know this part without needing to see it—forces the struggling man-child down, pins him, forces him to swallow the tranquilizers that are supposed to keep this from happening. The shouting, the cursing, the repeated sentences die down slowly. The wall vibrates as your father drags him to his room next to yours and puts him on his bed, takes away his shoes ("No kicking! Bad to kick Daddy! No kicking! I'm a bad boy to kick Daddy!"), and turns off the lights.

No one knocks on your door. You're old enough to take care of yourself. Your other sibling—ten, maybe eleven years old, an unimaginable age to you—is somewhere else. Or maybe in the bedroom across the hall. You know better than to open the door to look.

When the silence stays unbroken except for low murmuring on the other side of the wall as he rocks himself to sleep, you slide out from under the bed in the now-dark room. You crawl under the covers and squeeze your Teddy tight, his furry arms and legs frayed with your love. The cat slithers out and makes a watchful spot for herself on the bed's edge. And you eventually fall asleep, knowing that tomorrow, your parents will make you kiss your assailant's prickly cheek and tell him you love him.

* * *

That was my life up until age eighteen, never knowing whether I'd live out the night after coming home from school. My parents chose to keep my sibling with disabilities at home, turning down residential placements when I was young because "someone else needs it more." At every turn, they chose his well-being over mine despite his repeated attempts to murder me. They—and the professionals involved in his care at the time—claimed he "couldn't help" the violence because he "didn't understand." They chose his needs over my needs despite his repeated attempts at what I know as an adult were incestuous molestation, which I didn't dare tell them about for fear of being called a liar. Special education teachers witnessed one incident; they didn't intervene. (To be charitable, I think they were too shocked.)

My sibling was/is disabled, but *understood* using violence to get his way. He *understood* that trying to strangle his five- or six-year-old sister was wrong. As an adult, I understand now that his disabilities are not just autistic spectrum, but also psychotic. He was a danger to me, to my family, and potentially to people outside the household. The adults who were supposed to protect me as well as him refused to see that evidence before them. I was the youngest sibling; my other sibling, years older than I, also refused to see the evidence. My extended family turned a blind eye.

As a young adult—despite suffering from PTSD originating from my sibling's attacks on me—I was the one who made sure the arrangements for his residential placement were completed years before my last surviving parent died specifically so that my sibling would have time to adjust to a new home and there would be helping professionals present to ease that loss for him. My family gave me no credit. After my last parent died several years ago, my older sibling promptly disowned me for "not doing your fair share" with my brother and told me that the extended family agreed I shouldn't have been allowed to inherit because of it. Even though I'd been my last parent's primary caregiver and did *all* the executrix work that didn't focus on my sibling with disabilities specifically to ease the burden on my other sibling, none of that counted.

Why? I wasn't adhering to the familial party line of "You are not allowed to have a life of your own because you have a sibling with disabilities and your life was over before it began. You have to accept that martyrdom without complaint and without telling the truth about his violence."

I drew boundaries, supported by my therapist, in terms of caregiving. I was willing to handle paperwork for my brother so long as I never had to see him again and thus suffer the weeks of disabling panic attacks I get at even the *thought* of seeing him. My desperate need to set boundaries was enough for the remainder of my family to choose my sibling with disabilities over me. Again.

I understand some of why my parents made the choices they did: long before I was born, back in the days of Willowbrook, there *weren't* other good choices. My parents were in agony and they were trying to do the best they could for their child with disabilities. I have compassion for that even as I regret the destructive consequences to all of us of the choices they made and the denial into which they retreated.

But no one in my family or in the developmental disabilities profession had compassion for *me* as a child. No one protected *me*. It was made clear to me that my life had no value compared to that of my sibling with disabilities, that nothing I said about how he treated me would be believed, and that if he managed to kill me during one of those terrifying evenings he would never be punished.

As an adult, the only place where I have found any compassion or understanding is the Sibling Support Project. My hope in writing this essay and baring these wounds is to make it clear that the societal myth that Life Is Always Wonderful and Heartwarming with a Sibling with Disabilities is just that: a *myth*. The complex reality of having a sibling with disabilities may be ennobling for some, but for others—like me—it can be chaotic and violent. Acknowledging this truth does not demonize someone with disabilities, but protects both that person and the other people around him or her.

Even though I cannot be directly involved with my sibling, I do what I can in terms of advocacy for individuals with developmental disabilities. For me, that means advocating against common derogatory slurs such as "retard" used by both public figures and people in my private life. As a result, several people in my private life with no connection to the disability world have taken up the cause of advocating against these slurs. But otherwise, I am and will remain an "uninvolved sibling" because to be involved would cost me my sanity. That's too high a price to pay.

14.
Out of Sight, Out of Mind?

Kathy Coudle King

Out of sight, out of mind. That was a lot of people's philosophy back in the 1960s and '70s when I was growing up with my brother Jimmy in New Jersey. Why, our apartment's super had a son, Ronnie, who lived in an "institution." I'm sure lots of people in my neighborhood had a relative who had been "put away" because the family didn't think they could handle the daily care of the individual. But not my mom. I think Dad suggested it, but Mom refused.

When Jimmy lost his hearing and speech at the age of two after contracting the measles and running a high fever, he also suffered brain damage. Somewhere along the line he was diagnosed with autism, as well. And Jimmy was a handful. Stubborn? Oh, yeah. Obsessive-compulsive? You bet. But Mom kept him home with her, with us, and there he was from the moment I entered the world. My big brother was always there, and he was always on my mind.

I did the usual things kids do while growing up—had friends— just never brought them home. Participated in Girl Scouts and cheer-leading—just never had my family at events. Did Mom sense my embarrassment at having a brother with multiple disabilities—one who'd "whoop" and strike the air with his fist at inappropriate times. (Is there an appropriate time? Football games?) Or was she ashamed of his behavior and I absorbed this shame? Because shame it was. I was ashamed of Jimmy. There. I wrote it. (Can't quite say it, though.) I was ashamed and now I'm ashamed of my shame.

The funny thing about tucking Jimmy away at home or not mixing him with my community was that he was out of sight, but he was never far from my mind.

As far back as I can remember, like preschool age, I was terrified my mother was going to die. Most kids worry about losing their parents, sure, but my fear was linked with an almost palpable fear that I would be responsible for my brother. I had a sister, older, but somehow I always feared *I'd* be the one who would have to take Jimmy in. Mom and Dad never talked about it. Never assured me that they didn't expect me to or even that they expected me to. It was just one of the many things we never spoke about it in our house. But just because you don't talk about it, doesn't mean you don't think about it, and I *obsessed* about it throughout my life.

Moving 2000 miles away didn't help. Having four kids didn't help (hey, now I had a full house, "sorry, can't take him, no room!"). The time bomb that was RESPONSIBILITY was ticking. Mom had a bad heart. Dad passed in 1984. Mom refused to enroll Jimmy in even a daycare or respite program. He'd had no schooling, training, or even social interaction. What in the hell was I going to do when Mom died? Two thousand miles away and Jimmy was always on my mind.

Then it happened. Mom had a second heart attack. She was on life-support. Given a 10 percent chance to ever live on her own again. The perennial question hung in the hallways of the ICU: What were we going to "do" with Jimmy? Here my mother was on her deathbed and I was fixated on my brother. It should never have been like that. But that's what happens when people put things out of sight. They don't go away. They just wait; wait for the day when you can no longer pretend they don't exist. And there was Jimmy. Waiting for me to do something.

I did. We did. My sister and I. We found a group home, a wonderful group home, the kind of place I didn't even think existed. It was more than safe; it was a place where Jimmy could develop and finally assert his individuality. It was a place where he was encouraged to participate in household chores, to earn his first paycheck, to make friends—*for the first time in his fifty-one years.* He dressed up for Halloween and danced with a woman, he celebrated his hero Elvis's birthday by wearing shades and chops, "singing" into a microphone. He spent his own money at fairs; he made art, really great art, and—here's what really takes my breath away—he was learning sign language. Since food was always one of Jimmy's (and my) joys in life, it's no wonder that some of his first signs were for pizza and hamburger. I was told he not only knew the sign for "milk," but he was now recognizing the word on paper. The world of words was opening up to him, and I looked forward to my next visit when Jimmy would "talk" to me. What would he say? At last, Jimmy was neither out of sight nor out of mind.

And when, miraculously, my mother did not die (in fact, she now lives on her own) another miracle occurred: she accepted Jimmy's move to the group home. She recognized that it wasn't the 1960s any more. She recognized that there were others who could assist Jimmy. The son who was never far from her mind now lived a mile away, but he was not out of sight. He was an active member of a community, a community which even does fundraising for women's shelters.

Jimmy, my big brother, was finally out of the closet.

Then, suddenly, on March 3, 2007 he died. In his sleep. He was fifty-two years old. There are more than 2000 miles between us now. And you know what? He's on my mind every day. I see him in all the things he loved: John Wayne, old Hollywood musicals, *Star Trek,* Mexican food, a can of pop. I see him in the mirror and I see him in my sons. Out of sight, out of mind? Not when you're a sib. Never when you're a sib.

* * *

The youngest of three children, **Kathy Coudle King** *was born in West New York, New Jersey and graduated from N.Y.U.'s Dramatic Writing Program. She credits her love of theatre to her brother, who loved black-and-white musicals and movies. She holds an M.A. in English from the University of North Dakota, where she is a lecturer in English and Women Studies.*

A playwright, Kathy has written forty-plus plays. Seven were commissioned by nonprofits, and her plays have been produced at academic and medical conferences in addition to theatres in twelve states. Kathy believes in the power of theatre to reach audiences on a variety of issues. She worked with young sibs at her local Sibshop to write a short play with music called Is Anybody Out There? *She is happy to make it available for nonprofits interested in educating about the experience of sibs. Kathy is also the author of* Wannabe, *a coming-of-age novel (www.dakotalit.com).*

15.
The Chasm*

Antoinette Errante

> *"A bit of advice given to a young Native American*
> *at the time of his initiation:*
> *'As you go the way of life, you will come to a great chasm.*
> *Jump.*
> *'It is not as wide as you think.'"*
>
> — Joseph Campbell

It had been a wonderful day of blinking Christmas lights and Bing Crosby and the smell of roasts and sweets. The house was dark except for the lights on the Christmas tree and the one in my mother's kitchen where I was finishing up the dishes while my brother Bruno painted at the kitchen table. It had taken ten years, but the house finally smelled as if my mother was still with us, full of garlic and

---

* **chasm** Pronunciation:\•ka-z´m\, **1:** a deep cleft in the surface of a planet (as the earth)
: gorge **2:** a marked division, separation, or difference

cloves and steam from the clanging radiators. I felt so lucky to have my brother Bruno in my life. We were safe, happy.

When I think of the moments that have brought me the most pleasure, they are always connected to times when I felt like I had—even for an instant—kept my brother...safe. I dare you to find a picture of us as children where I don't have my arms around him. I was not always sure what he was in danger from, but it felt like he was so vulnerable. And that made me feel vulnerable. And it *still* makes me feel vulnerable.

But now the house was calm and we were sheltered from the world. I looked at Bruno as he painted, beautiful swirls of red and blue and purple and orange mixed with yellow. I watched as he would paint feverishly yet purposefully for a few seconds and then stop, tilt his head, and examine his composition before deciding which colors he needed next. I remember wishing for the confidence and faith he has. He seems to know exactly where to place his brush, and each stroke appears just as effortlessly as all the others before. The paintings he created that evening—one beautiful painting after another—were extraordinary.

He's remarkable, this brother of mine who was labeled "retarded," and who the doctors told my mother would be "spastic" and a "vegetable." He'll never speak, never walk. Never be a person is what they meant. Lock him up and have another baby, they said to her.

I remember the day my mother came screaming out of Willowbrook, shouting that they were all crazy and that she would never put her baby there. I was four years old and it was Halloween. I was dressed up as Little Red Riding Hood, a pumpkin basket in hand ready for trick-or-treat. That was the day I learned my brother was in danger because not everyone could see how extraordinary he was. And that was the day I learned *I* was in danger because not everyone could see how extraordinary my brother was.

But on this particular Christmas evening, in our mother's house, as I watched him paint, it was as if I were seeing him for the first time. Who was this person who painted so brilliantly? I leaned toward him; he scarcely noticed me. And I whispered in his ear, "Brother spirit, who are you?"

My brother looked up from his painting, and stared deeply into my eyes. And then he expressed his most profound thought: "BUUUUUUUUUUUUURP."

Aaaaaaaaaaaah. Now, we are Italian; everything is a sign. My best guess was my "brother spirit" was telling me to lighten up and not take everything so seriously. Life is supposed to be joyful and playful, not somber and dangerous. Well, I thought, that's easy for you to say, Bruno. (In truth, Bruno does not speak. But that has never stopped us from communicating.) And by the way, Bruno, the world *is* dangerous. It *is* somber. And what the heck is this thing called "play"? Who has ever had time to play? I've been too busy being the perfect-daughter-who-would-compensate-for-all-the-tragedy-in-the-house. Too busy playing St. Michael the Archangel (no, really, that's what I played when I was three and four) sent to protect you from all the bad people in the world. And we had met lots of bad people over the years.

Still, I thought, if God wants me to stop playing the boo-hoo version of my childhood rumbling around in my head and replace it with angelic harps playing an Aren't-We-A-Spiritual-Pair tape, I had to get real. And what is more real than a loud, satisfying burp?

So I took note of the sign, but mostly locked it away. But I did start to question the world a bit. Other people did not seem to walk around ever-alert that "danger" might be lurking around every corner. Then again, most other people are not guardians of a brother with a cognitive disability—and one who is nonverbal at that. When he was eight, Bruno could not tell you who had left him in the hall of his school alone, crying in pain from a mysteriously dislocated shoulder. Later, he came home from summer camps full of bruises and sores. And now I was his guardian, living in one city while Bruno lived in a group home in the city where we grew up. He had falls and fractures and infections and clothes stolen. As in childhood, he still needed protection.

You get the picture.

Still, I was afraid to move him closer. First of all, my mom had given the last ten years of her life to raising funds for the organization that ran his group home. She had done everything they say a parent should do to make sure Bruno would be well cared for and to assure that my needs would be considered as well. How could I possibly think of undoing all that hard work, just because the monthly trips to see Bruno were breaking my bank account and my spirit? And what if moving him closer did not work out? What if doing so left him even worse off? What if I can't find a place for him here? We have no other family. How will we make it? How can I work and support us and take care of him?

This was the danger, the thing that had terrorized me all of my life: Bruno. Me. Alone. And I can't keep him safe. It was a vision so terrible, an unknown so profound, the very thought made me feel like I would fall off the end of the earth. And so for many years, there was no leap of faith because there was no faith.

This is the story of how I leapt across my personal chasm.

Do you know the scene in the movie *It's a Wonderful Life,* where you watch the earth spin as if from the vantage point of God, and you hear heavenly voices discussing what they were going to do for poor George Bailey? Well, I figure a similar conversation took place about me between (let's say) God and my guardian angel. Let's include St. Michael the Archangel, too, since he and I go way back.

GOD: Well, I have sent Antoinette just about as many signs as I could send—without showing up in person—to let her know that she needs to get Bruno closer to her. Look at how miserable they both are so far apart from each other.

GUARDIAN ANGEL: I've tried my best to whisper words of encouragement. And I have even whispered advice into her friends' ears so that she could hear it from them. But she answers every piece of advice with another fear, another "what if…." She's wearing me out.

ST. MICHAEL: It is looking pretty hopeless, God. I can't even begin to penetrate the wall of fear she's built around herself to give her a shot of faith and courage. She has no idea I am even around!

GOD: We tried the easy way by laying the whole path out in front of her, and by bringing people into her life who could help her and lead the way. But she's not getting it! There's only one way to help her now. I am going to have to resort to…

GOD, ST. MICHAEL, AND GUARDIAN ANGEL *(in unison):* The HARD WAY!

So, Bruno was set to come for a thirty-day visit over the summer. I had arranged appointments to meet with my county board of MRDD to see about transferring Bruno. I now laugh at how foolish I was to think this would be an easy transition: you know, find a place here, pack up Bruno's belongings, and presto, just move him without him ever losing a day of services. Keep my fears of the unknown at bay.

Who knew about waiting lists? Who knew he would never be eligible for the Medicaid that would ultimately make him eligible for services until he had surrendered his Medicaid elsewhere and established a new residence? Who knew "the system" was designed so that I would have to make hundreds of choices about programs and service providers who were not obligated to publish any information about the quality of their record?

Poor me. So utterly ignorant....

So I flew to pick Bruno up and then flew back with him. Bruno *loves* to fly and we had a great trip. But by that first evening, I noticed he was more lethargic than usual. His breathing was unusually heavy during the night. By the following morning, he was having trouble breathing.

By the following nightfall, he had been admitted to the hospital with severe double pneumonia.

By the middle of the week, on the very day we were supposed to be meeting to discuss Bruno's move, Bruno was intubated.

Respiratory failure.

Sepsis.

Medically induced coma.

Prepare yourself, the doctors told me. There is a very good chance your brother will not survive.

But I was not prepared. I crumbled and sobbed, sobbed, sobbed. Who would I love? Who would love me? And then, through my sobbing, I heard a whisper, "Have some faith. This pneumonia is about to be the best thing to happen to Bruno." Oh no, I thought, I am losing my grip....

My friend Katie came to spend that first of many nights with me. I could not sleep, fearing at any moment I would get a call that my brother....

But I finally fell asleep, and when I awoke and realized no one had called, I dared to hope a little.

Katie and I went to the hospital. My brother was swollen and bruised, tubes everywhere. I crumbled. In my head I began making funeral arrangements. And then I heard Katie whisper in my ear, "Antoinette, keep talking to him. Look, his blood pressure goes up when you talk to him." Katie kept whispering, "Don't give up. Bruno's tough. Come on, let's go get his CD player and some of his favorite music."

Ten days in intensive care.

Thirty days on a step-down floor.

He would need a rehab facility.

So I said to myself, OK, this must be a sign that Bruno is not to ever go back.

And so, providence did what I could not have done alone: get Bruno closer to me. It would be over a year before I would finally find a place Bruno could really call home and a day program that fills him with friendship and wonder.

And during the year that was my chasm, I faced a thousand tiny fears I had saved up since I was three and told my mother I wanted to be a police officer just to arrest the people who had done this to my brother:

- Fears about having enough money. Somehow a check, a credit to my bank account would show up when I needed it.
- Fears about not being able to care for Bruno. My friend Barbara had planned to live with me while her house was being restored. The restoration that was to take a few months took over a year. In the end, Barbara moved out just as we found Bruno a wonderful residence. All my friends pitched in during the year Bruno spent every day with me because I could not bear to leave him in a nursing home with lovely people but no activities or friends. But Barbara saved my life. She washed, bathed, fed, played, and loved so much my brother

began to get fed up having two women hugging and kissing him all the time.

- Fears I had no family. I found that families are made from the heart, not from blood.
- Fears that my fear would kill me. I am still here.

I came to my chasm. And I jumped. OK, let's say I was pushed. But I learned that the chasm was not all that wide and that liberation was waiting for me on the other side. There will be good days and bad days. Sometimes, I am still afraid. But the fear of what awaits me in the future no longer paralyzes my present. I can enjoy the sweet smile my brother gives me. It's a smile so full of love it makes others jealous because no one looks at them that way. And when his mood shifts and he begins banging imperiously on the table for his dinner, I can happily fantasize about leaving him on a stranger's doorstep. I can savor each moment. The unnamed dread that has haunted me for four decades has finally been put to rest. I can do *anything* now.

Anything at all....I am relishing the possibilities.

Wow. And here I thought I was born to ensure Bruno lived up to his full potential. Maybe it's been the other way around all along....

* * *

Antoinette Errante lives in Columbus, Ohio, where she is an Associate Professor of Educational Policy and Comparative Education at Ohio State University. When not with her brother and friends or tending to her garden, she can often be found in Mozambique and South Africa, where she has learned from traditional healers and war-affected communities how to work for peace.

16.
I'm Still Learning How to Take Care of Myself

Yasuko Arima

"Where did you go during holidays?" classmates or coworkers would ask me.

My answer was "Nowhere." The conversation ended.

I grew up in a typical nuclear family—albeit a Japanese family living in the Tokyo metropolitan area. I have two sisters—one younger and one older. My younger sister, Momoko, has cerebral palsy and has lived in a facility for people with severe physical and intellectual disabilities since 1988. She is bedridden, uses a wheelchair, and needs total care.

Her disabilities weren't always that severe. Momoko's cerebral palsy was mild at birth. Then, when she was two years old, she got pneumonia and was unconscious for about a week. She lost a lot of abilities. However, she gradually regained an ability to express herself. Now we can infer how she feels from her facial expression and vocalizations. She loves lively music and toys that makes sounds.

I have only vague memories of my childhood, but my most vivid memory is my desire to have a younger sibling. Consequently, when

Momoko was born, I was ecstatic and loved to help care for her. I wrote about my dream to become a doctor in a collection of commemorative compositions by students graduating from my elementary school. I don't know whether my parents took this seriously, but because of Momoko's disability, my parents decided I should become a doctor and work at the facility where my sister would live. They decided what path I would take.

The dream to become a doctor and to take care of my sister's daily needs reflected my deep love for Momoko. However, as I grew older, my world became bigger. In dealing with my wider world of friends and classmates, unconsciously, I repressed my desires. I would frequently break promises with my friends, because I had to look after the house and my sister or go shopping for daily necessities. I had few friends. One day, one of my friends sprained her ankle and she asked me to go to a hospital with her. I promised I would do it, but I had to look after the house on that day and had to break my promise. She got angry. This memory still causes me sorrow.

Because of the expectations my parents and I had about my future, I was forced to go to cram schools for math and English to study for entrance examinations for the medical department in university. I was twelve years old and in seventh grade at the time.

I don't remember when it started, but I eventually complained about my situation and not being free to go out when I wanted to. My mother, who also suppressed her desire for freedom, would say, "You should control your desire to go out and remember you can walk and go anywhere you want—unlike your sister."

When I was a university student, I planned a getaway with a guy I liked and other friends during Golden Week, five consecutive holidays in May. I've never forgotten my mother's response: "Are you going out in spite of your sister and your responsibility to her on these holidays?" I did go out, but I could not suppress the feeling that I had no right to live my own life.

When entrance examinations to universities approached, I was crushed by the pressure to become a doctor from my parents and the realities of Japanese society. A woman working outside of the home is not something that is generally accepted. I had to study very hard and

I was not allowed to meet friends, see movies, or go out. I was forced to study so much that I lost my direction and forgot why I wanted to become a doctor. I failed my entrance examinations in the first year and studied to take them again for the following year. After all of this, I entered a university where I studied environmental science.

My parents discouraged me—and my older sister—from marrying. They said, "You won't be able to get married because of Momoko's disabilities, so you must support yourselves." Eventually, I chose to remain a single person after I encountered the feminist movement and learned the history of the Japanese family system. But I still resented my parents' advice not to marry. And, it was great comfort when I met siblings who were single and had no kids on SibNet, the U.S.-based listserv for adult sibs. I was grateful for the opportunity to meet them, because I had only met two Japanese feminists who are "siblings" and we never talked about sibling issues.

To really understand the issues faced by adult sisters of people with disabilities in Japan, it helps to know about the historical Japanese concept of "family." The most common Japanese term for family is *ie*, a Confucian term often translated as "household." *Ie* was organized as a hierarchy with the male head of the household at the apex, in a position of absolute authority. This authority was supported by law until the end of World War II. A bride of any son traditionally holds the lowest status in the *ie*, and a bride of the eldest son might be divorced if she fails to please her in-laws or produce a healthy boy.

Today, thanks to changes made to the Japanese constitution following World War II, women are less restricted to the home and are freer to pursue education and jobs, and to initiate divorce. Despite such rapid change, however, the concept of *ie* remains in the civil law and deeply in the Japanese psyche. A bride, for instance, can be forced to care for her husband's aging parents. Consequently, if a woman marries an eldest son, there is every possibility that she won't be able to take care of her own aging parents—not to mention a sibling who has a disability.

The message I was given early in life was that my needs were less important than others'. And considering my own needs only made me feel guilty. To make matters worse, I was trapped in an abusive relationship with a boyfriend during my twenties and thirties. My inability to put my own needs first kept me in this relationship for years.

With colleagues, I created an adult sibling group in Tokyo in 1998. Then, in 2005, we adapted recovery programs intended for adult children of alcoholics. From these programs we learned that children who grow up in environments where it is unsafe to be a child or there are too many responsibilities often learn to act in ways that are beyond their developmental ages. They become an "adult" as a child, and often function as a "little child" in adult life. Later, I discovered Julie Tallard Johnson's book *Hidden Victims/Hidden Healer: An Eight-Stage Healing Process for Family and Friends of the Mentally Ill.* Finally, I began to realize that I could be a caregiver—but not a caretaker. Caregivers take care of themselves first even while they provide support and nurturing to others. Caretakers are those who put others' wants and needs before their own.

I became Momoko's legal guardian when our father passed away in 2002. Since she needs total care, it would be easy to become a caretaker, but much harder to become a caregiver. So my biggest challenge is how to maintain a "delicate balance" so I can meet both my own needs and Momoko's needs.

Unfortunately, Momoko's swallowing ability is declining. Some staff members of the facility where she lives suggested a feeding tube. This suggestion upset my mother and me and we met with the staff in 2006. They seemed to understand our concerns and switched Momoko to more pureed food rather than a feeding tube.

Forty-five years ago, the Japanese government told parents of people with severe physical and intellectual disabilities that there was no money to spend on "useless" people. Parents' persistent lobbying influenced governmental policies, and services have improved over the years. However, because of national financial difficulties, the government wants to reduce the cost of welfare and medical insurance. One way to accomplish this goal was found in a law enacted in 2006. This law stresses that families should support people with disabilities financially and people with disabilities should find a way to support themselves.

This new initiative not only reminds elderly parents of the past discriminatory words and attitude of the government but sends a potentially frightening message to adult siblings. Some people with disabilities who live in the community with assistance from home helpers have had to fight to keep their current level of services. And some people with mild disabilities have lost their jobs. A local facility for people with severe physical and intellectual disabilities had to reduce the number of people they could serve, and twelve people were suddenly without a home.

Given these circumstances, my biggest issue now is knowing whether I will have enough time to attend to Momoko's needs when my mother is no longer around. I love my sister, but I don't want to give up my life to care for her.

My desire to care for my sister—and still attempt to lead as normal a life as possible—has already required changes. My previous job was as an editor at a nonprofit society for preservation of wildlife. Because it required long working hours and paid poorly, I changed jobs and went into the medical field. But there was another reason for changing jobs: Japan is far behind the United States in providing siblings with support. I have learned so much from English-language publications and English-speaking people. I wanted a job requiring English and medical knowledge to improve my English skills and advocate for my sister. I also moved closer to Momoko's facility. But, commuting time remains an issue, so I continue to hunt for a job that will allow me to be even closer to her.

The facility where Momoko lives is not paradise, but Momoko has gone on trips to museums and to a famous zoo. These are experiences she never would have had if she had remained in our family's home. Because she's at the facility, I have freedom to go out—even go abroad—though I still feel guilty occasionally. And most importantly, if there had not been the facility, we (our mother, my older sister, and myself) would never have survived our father's serious illness.

"Where did you go during holidays?" Coworkers ask.

My answers have changed.

"I went to Seattle and Boston to meet my friends from SibNet and to New York to attend sibling sessions at an international conference."

Now that I have the support of other siblings and a little bit of freedom, I find I can be more open to these sorts of questions. Things still aren't perfect with Momoko, and maybe never will be. But now, at least, I am learning to take care of myself.

* * *

Yasuko Arima was born in Kanagawa Prefecture, Japan, in 1962. Upon graduation from university, she was briefly involved in Japan's feminist movement. In 1997, she discovered the Sibling Support Project on the Internet and has brought the project director to Japan twice for workshops and training on the Sibshop model. She has been a facilitator of a sibling support group for adults since 1998 and has run the Sibling Support Awareness Group with colleagues since 2004. With the help of mothers from the Japan Hydrocephalus Association, Yasuko started a Sibshop for kids whose siblings had hydrocephalus in 2006. She majored in environmental science at university, but after many twists and turns, she currently works at a pharmaceutical company as an indexer of a medical database. Her present goal is to become a medical translator. She likes nature walks, especially bird watching.

17.
Walkout

Veronica Chater

[Transcript from Chicago Public Radio's This American Life]

Ira Glass, host of *This American Life:* Veronica Chater's younger brother Vincent can't do math, even the simplest addition. He doesn't speak well. He has a version of what used to be called mental retardation. But when he was a baby, and doctors tried to diagnose him, they couldn't find anyone else with his particular combination of symptoms, so they named his own syndrome after him…the Vincent Syndrome. He's an adult now, and for a while seemed to be doing just fine…until last year…when he surprised everyone in the family by quitting his job. By quitting everything, in fact.

And it wasn't clear to them why he did it…and what it meant. And how he would live if he'd continue to refuse to work. Veronica Chater put together this story.

©Veronica Chater. Originally broadcast on *This American Life,* produced by Chicago Public Radio.

Veronica: Ever since Vincent quit his job, he's spent more and more time alone in his room.

At Christmas at our parents' house in Northern California, my brothers and sisters and I weave in and out of the kitchen, talking about work, telling jokes and taking orders from Mom. There are eleven of us. I'm the second oldest; Vinny's the fifth.

As usual, he's nowhere to be seen. When I go down the hall I find him in his bedroom with the door closed drinking an orange soda from the can, and watching an old movie.

Tape: *rich orchestration and dialogue from 1939 version of* Wuthering Heights

His face is close to the TV screen, about ten inches away, and he has a serious expression —the kind you'd catch on a detective who's trying to crack a case.

He could be eighteen and he could be fifty. But you can't quite tell. He has a short, little boy haircut and every day wears a sweatshirt with the words "Carpe Diem" on it. The truth is, he's thirty-four.

Tape:
> **Veronica:** *Did Santa come and fill your stocking?*
> **Vinny:** *Indeed*
> **Veronica:** *What did you get in your stocking?*—
> **Vinny:** *Envelopes…address book…and jamaroonies*
> **Veronica,** *laughing: Jamaroonies?*

Vinny still lives in his childhood bedroom. Which he calls his apartment. The walls are decked out with animal posters and his bed is covered with a Scooby Doo comforter. On his dresser are dozens of trophies and medals that he's won over the years—at various bowling tournaments and Special Olympics events.

Ever since he retired, bit by bit he's been withdrawing into his own little world, a world that doesn't include me or anyone else.

* * *

Tape: *sound of electric razor*
   Mom: *OK, here you go, we'll clean you up.*

My mom and dad still take care of Vinny. But it's mainly my mom's job.

Tape:
   Vinny: *Clean you, clean you.*
   Mom: *Shave ya, shave ya.*

My parents, who are devout Roman Catholics, were undaunted by the idea of having a so-called "special needs child." They figured it was part of God's plan: he was an angel in our midst, as my dad always said. They refused to think of him as a burden, even though he would depend on them for the rest of their lives.

Every morning my Mom readies him for the day. Combing and gelling hair, brushing his teeth. And shaving him.

Tape: *sound of electric razor:*
   Mom, *singing: I like my clean-shaven man!*

She tilts his chin this way and that, handling him like a barber with an overbooked schedule.

Tape:
   Mom: *Done...all spiffed up for the day...put your shaver away.*
   Vinny: *Here we go!*

There are all sorts of little games Vinny and my mom play together, all day long. Most of them are impenetrable to outsiders. He'll say "repeat, repeat" and she'll reply "redeep in the redeep" and they'll both giggle.

Tape: *guitar music in background*
   Mom: *OK, I'm going to test you. I want to see if you know any movies because you're the one who always knows movies. Who sucked his thumb and said "Mommy!!"*

Vinny: The cartoon Robin Hood!

Mom: Right! You got that! I didn't know if you were going to get that!

Despite his disability, Vinny has a really good memory for all sorts of trivia—sports facts, dates, movie titles. Quizzing him about movies is the impromptu game my mom and dad play with him throughout the day from morning till night.

Tape:

> *Dad: I've got one for you, Vincent. See if you can get this. (Singing) "Hitch was up Monday, Ain't gonna soldier no more."*

The bond between them is more than a bond—it's a union for life. As Vinny passed through his teenage years and became an adult, Mom saw to it that he was kept busy. She signed him up for bowling, for Special Olympics, and for pretty much every seasonal sport, from basketball to badminton.

But as he got older, Vinny's personality grew darker, and more mysterious. I didn't notice it right away. I don't think any of us did. Mom was so good at keeping Vinny distracted from himself that it didn't seem like a problem. But two years ago it grew too large to ignore.

Tape:

> *Vinny: Let's play games.*
>
> *Mom: I'm not playing games right now. Go get my sour cream! (laughing) Come on, I want the sour cream. I can't make those Chantilly potatoes without it!*

Every time I go home it hits me a little bit more, that even though Vincent and I are about the same age, my mom talks to him like he's a precocious four-year-old. And more and more I've noticed that he's aware of it too. When he returned without the sour cream, and noticed that mom and I were talking about him...he got upset.

Tape:

Vinny: Is that a wonderful reaction to talk about someone when you talk about me I wonder?

Mom: I was talking right in front of you. I wasn't telling any secrets. I'm going to say what I am going to say because it's true! Nothing wrong with having the truth, is there?

Vinny leaves.

Mom: Dad is so afraid he's going to get him angry he won't give him any orders. I have to give him all the orders. If he wants to get smart with me and I say "God said you have to obey your parents; I'm your mother you do what I say when I say." And he'll do something sometime and I'll say you go in your room and tell God you're sorry for that. He'll go in his room and come out and say "I'm sorry for talking like that." I'll said that's fine, Vin, OK. We just don't do that. And then he gets in a really good mood after that.

It might seem like my mom is rough on Vinny—but I have to say that her way of dealing with him has pretty much worked out for the best. Until the day Vinny decided to retire.

When he quit his job, Vinny dropped *everything*—including bowling, basketball, and the Special Olympics. Where once he was busy from dawn till dusk, now he had nothing to do. So he began sleeping to pass the time…up to eighteen hours a day.

It worried all of us, especially Mom. He was sleeping his life away and we didn't understand why. It felt like we were losing him. Like he was giving up.

And so I set out to figure out why.

If you ask Vinny about why he quit his job, you don't get much of an answer. In general, it's hard to get a direct response out of him on any subject. "Could be," he'll say. Or "Maybe." It's not clear he even knows what his own feelings are sometimes. Often when any of us asks about his job, he'll just change the subject, like he did when I asked him about it in Mom's kitchen.

Tape:

Veronica: How come you just won't tell me why you quit?

Vinny: "*Mysteriously it might be empty, blank in there, after you were saying something.*"

Veronica: You mean you're leaving that section blank because you don't want to fill it in with words?

Vinny: Blank is there before I finish words.

Veronica: Are you playing word games with me now?

Vinny: No.

We've all asked Vinny dozens of times, in dozens of different ways, why he quit his job and everything else, and every time his answer is just as cryptic. And so, we're all forced to guess what the real reasons are.

My mom's best guess is that Vinny put himself into early retirement…and started with all these dark moods…because of a chemical change in his brain.

Tape: sounds of food cooking in background

Mom: The psychologist said he thinks it was a chemical imbalance that took place suddenly in his brain and he prescribed Prozac for him.

Veronica: It's all chemical?

Mom: I don't know. It's really a mystery to me what happened.

Vinny had worked for twelve years at a place called Concord Support Services—a company that hires mentally retarded adults and vocationally trains them.

Vinny always told me that he liked his job. He'd sit in a big warehouse with about sixty other disabled adults doing light assembly or stuffing envelopes. He made up to sixty dollars a month. Which to him was an infinite amount of money.

We all assumed he'd found his place in the world. Then, gradually, he started to become impatient and angry at work, threatening to break people's fingers if they touched him. He started disappearing into the work bathroom for up to an hour at a time—just to get away from people. It was pretty clear that he was in a crisis.

On his last day, he was wandering around, looking for a bead he'd dropped. His supervisor asked him what he was doing. One thing led to another, Vinny lost his temper, my parents were called in for a meeting, and Vinny quit. Just up and walked out.

Tape: *music break*

A few months ago, I asked Vinny if he'd like to go back to his old job just for a visit, hoping it might spark something. I wasn't sure how he'd react. But he didn't even hesitate. He told me that he'd love to go. So the next morning, after my mom spiffed him up, we drove the route he'd taken for twelve years. When we arrive at the front doors he's all smiles, he seems genuinely glad to be there.

But as we approach the warehouse floor where Vinny used to work, his pace slows. At the warehouse door he hesitates and purses his lips together.

Tape: *(lots of people talking)*
    Vinny: *Hi.*
    Man: *How are you?*
    Vinny: *Wonderful, how nice to see you.*
    Woman: *How you doing?*
    Vinny: *Wonderful. Nice pretty pins.*
    Woman: *Thank you.*

He becomes shy and looks confused as one person after another comes up to him. Some touch him fondly; one man blows in his face, and everyone stares. Vinny tries to appear cool, but I can tell he's tense.

Tape:
    Man: *We miss you, Vinny. We miss the Vinny we knew. We missed you.*
    Vinny: *Would you like to begin basketball practice?*
    Man: *I don't know. I'm back into bowling and running again.*

We hang out and Vinny looks uncomfortable except when he decides, on his own, to busy himself cleaning and straightening. After fifteen minutes, he disappears into the bathroom, his old hiding place. After a while, he comes out for a few minutes, then goes back in, and then comes back out again. When he heads back into the bathroom for the third time, I know it's time to leave.

Later I talk to my brother Danny about it. Of all my siblings, Danny spends the most time with Vinny. They go to movies, take walks, go to bookstores. Danny thinks Vinny might've quit his job for all the normal reasons any of us quit a job. Maybe it had nothing to do with his disability.

Tape:
 Danny: *I think he was extremely bored working in this place, doing the same thing over and over again. Stuffing envelopes, putting paper clips in bags. There was no challenge to it and I think it really frustrated him.*

Vinny might have simply had enough. Enough of other people controlling his life. All the adults in his life were doing the sensible things you do for disabled people…giving structure to his days, coaxing his moods, all with the best of intentions…it's possible that in the end, that wasn't enough of a life. And so one day he changed the one thing in his life that he could, he said no to the one thing he could say no to, and quit his job. And then quit everything else.

Tape:
 Danny: *Being told what to do day in and day out, watching his other brothers and sisters, running around, and here he is, stuck in his room. It would make me angry being in that situation.*
 Music break indicating new scene

After Vinny retired, my mom and dad were determined to get him back into some kind of routine. After meeting with all sorts of social workers, and suggesting dozens of ideas to Vinny, they finally came up with something that he agreed to. She hired my brother Bernard to build a chicken coop in the backyard, and to put Vinny in charge of a miniature chicken farm. My mom had always wanted a chicken farm, anyway. This was her big chance to get one.

Vinny took to every aspect of chicken farming: he was pains-takingly mindful of the chickens' daily schedule of free-range feed-ing and lock-up, and he was especially fastidious about coop hygiene. But more than that: to everyone's surprise he started participating in activities again. He started basketball practice, and he's training again for the Special Olympics.

Tape: *Chicken sounds*
　　Vinny: *Molly, Polly, Janette, Marnie!*

Pretty much at any time of the day you can see Vinny stand-ing as still as a marble sculpture in the backyard beside the coop, his eyes half-closed and his palms cupping the breeze, thinking, or just listening to the sounds of his hens. He named them after old friends, and talks to them like children.

Tape:
　　Vinny: *Molly, Polly, Janette, Marnie!*
　　Chicken sounds

Right now he just has four chickens. Come spring, Mom's or-dering a dozen more for him. He's excited about that.

Tape: *More chickeny sounds…*

* * *

Veronica Chater's stories on her family have appeared in a variety of magazines, newspapers, anthologies, and radio, including This American Life. Her memoir, entitled Waiting for the Apocalypse, *about her Catholic family fleeing modern America to live in a rustic village in Portugal only to return penniless and disillusioned, will be published in February 2009 by W.W. Norton. Veronica lives with her documentary filmmaker husband, John Chater, and their three sons in Berkeley, California. You can visit her at www.veronicachater.com. Veronica's sister, Tarri, writes about her life with Vinnie in the essay "A Break for Freedom," found on page 123.*

18.
The Thirty-Nine Steps of Visiting Jon

Jennifer Owensby

I've been pretty stressed out for the past few months, for different reasons. My husband, Sweetie John (to distinguish from the other important Jon in my life), has been traveling weekly with his work as a network sports cameraman. And I have been traveling doing speaking engagements with my documentary, *The Teachings of Jon.* I made the documentary to explain how having my brother Jon in the family has been the best thing to ever happen to us. Because whenever I told people about Jon and that he is severely affected by Down syndrome, has an IQ of twenty, and doesn't talk, all they would say is, "I'm sorry." I admit Jon is on the low end of the totem pole, even for someone with Down syndrome. Even still, when I would introduce them to Jon, they didn't see his interesting way of relating or his great sense of humor or the tremendous joy and meaningfulness we found as a family. All they saw was burden. I made the film to try to change that perception. Now that it has been airing on public television all over the country, my life has become very busy and I'm still learning how to adjust to it.

In between traveling and working, Sweetie John and I have been designing and building our first house. Last week we had some deadlines with the house plans. I was becoming more and more stressed out about things like the rooflines, and the feng shui for the correct position of the stove, and whether the square footage was too much, or too little, and how much this is going to cost, and on and on. I started noticing how irritable I felt and how edgy and short I was acting. I thought maybe it's PMS. And then I realized, I'm needing a Bubby visit. That's Jon, my "Bubby."

I call Sandra, Jon's caretaker. "Hey Sandra, how's Bubby?" Sandra answers in her long southern drawl, "He's doing great. Watchin' *Batman* for the thousandth time. I wish I could get him to watch a different movie, you know, just for a change. I know this one by heart now!" I ask if tomorrow would be a good day to visit Jon. "Oh, you know he'd love to see you. He's doing so good, Jenny. You're going to be so proud of him. Do you know what he did last week? All by himself? With no prompting whatsoever?"

"What?" I'm waiting with bated breath.

"He washed his hands after he went potty! That's right. He sure did. All by himself." Sandra is just perfect for Jon. She too knows how to celebrate even the smallest of successes.

"That is so great, Sandra." She's right, I am proud of Bubby. That's taken forty years to accomplish!

"You want to talk to Jon?"

"Oh yes."

Conversations with Jon are a little one-sided since he doesn't talk. He'll slap his chest, point, make noises; somehow he definitely gets his point across. I hear, "Jon, it's Jenny. Jenny's on the phone." Then, with *Batman* in the background, I hear some heavy breathing. "Hey, Bubby. I love you. I miss you. I'm gonna come see you tomorrow!" Then I hear a telephone button being pushed. "Beep." I press the button once. "Beep." Then I hear the telephone button being pushed twice. "Beep...Beep." I push the button twice. "Beep... Beep." Then I only hear *Batman* in the background and some breathing. "Hey, Bubby, I'll see you tomorrow. I love you!"

Then I hear Sandra, "Did you hear that?" "What?" "He was kissin' and lovin' the phone. He always does that when you call!" Then I hear, "SLAP, SLAP!" "What is it, Jon? What do you want? Oh, your ears? Okay." Then to the phone, "Jon's wantin' some new ears."

"Okay, you tell him I'll bring him some new ears!" The "ears" are AM/FM stereo headphones, Jon's favorite. He loves his "ears." But he also has a particular knack for destroying them. Hence, the need for some new ones. No problem. I'll stop by Radio Shack on my way out.

Then I hear Sandra say so patiently, "Jenny said she's gonna bring you some new ears, Jon. That's right, Jenny's gonna bring 'em. That's right." Then back to the phone, "He's so happy you're coming. Oh yeah, there's one more thing he needs, an orange comb. The wide-tooth kind. But it has to be orange. Just like the one you brought him last time. That's his favorite. And he gets so mad at me when I can't find it! I only have one orange one, and he doesn't like any other color right now."

"Okay, I'll bring some new ears and an orange comb."

The Prep

The next morning I drop Sweetie John off at the airport. "Don't forget to Bubby-proof the truck," he says. That means to put away everything within reach, take down the good luck charm hanging from the rearview mirror that our friend Giorgio gave us, and absolutely put away all papers, receipts, etc. "And try not to leave him in the truck alone because you know he'll spit." Every once in a while I step back and wonder what this must sound like to others. We kiss good-bye and I drive to the Radio Shack.

I walk in and head straight for the stereo headphones, but the kind Jon likes is missing. I ask the manager. He says they're currently out of stock and shows me a smaller, flimsier set. Those won't work. "Would you please call another store to find who may have them in stock?" He doesn't understand. Not bringing the exact ears Jon wants after I promised him is just not an option. Jon doesn't understand "Sorry, they were out of stock." I am prepared to drive all over town to get Jon's ears if necessary.

Perhaps the manager senses my clear purpose that failure is just not an option here. "Maybe there are some in the new shipment. Wait one minute." I sigh in relief. He walks back with the perfect ears. "Oh, thank you very much. No other pair would have worked. Any chance they're on sale?" "Only if you get six or more." "I'm sure I've bought at least six. I buy these all the time." "You get them for your brother, don't you? Yes, I remember you. I'll give you a discount."

That's one of the ways Jon's magic works. People remember him and he brings out their kindness and generosity. That has happened my whole life. I remember when I sold Girl Scout cookies and took him around with me in his favorite little red wagon. He loved to be pulled in that red wagon and I took him everywhere and he brought me good luck too. I was amazed at how many boxes of cookies I sold!

I thank the manager and head next door to Sally's Beauty Supply with the same determination and purpose, to get what Jon wants—the orange wide-tooth comb. I go to the comb aisle and see that they don't have the exact orange comb I got him last time. There is a package with a blue comb and a smaller orange one. Then there are two other orange combs, one a wide-tooth pick, and the other a small pocket comb. Oh, what the heck, I'll take them all. That's three different orange combs and a blue one. Hopefully, Jon will like one of these.

Last stop, Food Lion. They have the best price on Epsom salts and they're right next door. They only have six half-gallon boxes; I buy them all. Jon loves his baths. And now that I got him hooked on Epsom salts and lavender essential oils, it has become a basic need. That's okay; I bring them every time I come. I already have the lavender essential oil packed in my bag.

Finally, it's time to hit the road if I want to get to Sandra's by 4:30. I like the three-and-a-half-hour drive. It gives me a chance to be quiet and think about all the things stressing me out.

The Arrival

When I arrive at Sandra's, I quickly "Bubby-proof" the truck. I put away the lucky charm, and make sure there are no business cards, car registration, or other important receipts or papers out in the open. I get his new "ears" and combs and walk up to Sandra's little house. "Jon's been so excited to see you, he's been sittin' at the window waitin' for you with his shoes and pants on." That is serious. He has to really want to see you to keep his pants and shoes on. I'm touched. I lean over and give him a big hug hello.

Sitting there in his Mickey Mouse t-shirt and only four feet tall, you'd never guess Jon is forty-seven years old. With his typical Down syndrome features of the almond-shaped eyes, round face, and little Buddha belly, he exudes the innocence of a toddler. "Oh yeah, he even packed all his things himself," Sandra adds. Jon has everything packed in his lunchbox—his Furby, his Wuv Luv (similar to Furby), his old earphones, and the orange comb. These must be with him at all times everywhere he goes.

"Hey Bubby, I brought you presents." He lights up. "You want to see what I brought you?" He knows what it is. "Some new ears!" He happily opens the box and immediately puts them on his head. "And look, Jon, I got you some orange combs!" He pulls them out of the bag and starts combing his stomach with one. Then he takes his old ears out from the lunchbox he packed and puts his new ears and combs in and zips it up. He stands, ready to go.

"Wait, Jon we still have to get your clothes out of the dryer," Sandra says ever so patiently. She pulls the clothes out of the dryer, folds them, and puts them into a bag. Jon grows impatient and roars. He is ready to be with just me. "He's talking a lot more these days," Sandra exaggerates.

"Talking?" I ask with a bit of sarcasm.

"Well, he's making more noises. I think he's trying to talk," she says, ever hopeful. Sandra has been amazing for Jon. He stays with her five nights a week now. And she's been able to get him to lose forty-five pounds! He used to look like a miniature sumo wrestler; now he just looks miniature. He is much more active, and now apparently more vocal.

"Sandra, I hate to dip into your stash, but can I take some of your foldin'?" I forgot his folding paper. How could I forget that?! It was in a bag near the front door. A nice thick pile of used 8 ½-by-11 paper for Jon to fold. I'd been saving it for a couple of weeks.

"Sure, I just got a box at your parents' yesterday."

Scrap paper is a valuable commodity at my parents' house. Luckily, their good friend, another John, volunteers at the local hospital press room, and brings Jon boxes of scrap paper every week. What a wonderful gift, since folding paper is his favorite activity.

Jon slaps his chest and grunts loudly. "Okay, Bubby, we're going!" He hands me his lunchbox to carry for him, takes my other hand and we walk slowly to the truck. Sandra wheels his wheelchair over with a large stack of paper in it, and puts it in the back.

Driving with Jon

Jon loves our new truck. He adjusts the seat so that it is all the way forward and the back is straight up. Lucky for him, he has very short legs; otherwise this arrangement would be very uncomfortable. But he's always done that. Sandra walks up and opens his door and he gives her a big hug. The kind where he messes up her hair and loves her up like he loves his Furby. I feel a little jealous at how much he loves her, but at the same time am so happy that he has her.

"Alright, Sandra, we'll see you tomorrow." Jon gives her the "I love you" sign and we head over to the Highland Lake Inn. That's where we stay when I visit. It's nearby, on fifty-some acres, has a great swimming pool, and it gives us a chance to hang out together, just my Bubby and me.

We're barely a block away when Jon starts adjusting the radio to the right song. Jon hits the buttons until he finds a song he likes. Then the air-conditioning controls. He likes the levers to be flush to the right. Unfortunately, that's the heat position and he doesn't understand why hot air is coming out. "Jon, that's the heat; we want the air-conditioning," I say as I move the controls to the left. He doesn't like that and moves them back to the right. "It's hot, Jon!" Oh well, sometimes you just have to let things go.

So we proceed up the mountain with the hot air blasting, the hazards blinking, the radio on rap music—very loud—and now he wants to adjust his seat yet again. It's been about twenty-five minutes since picking him up and that initial excitement of seeing him is already beginning to wear off. By this time I'm losing my patience and raising my voice, "Jon, will you just calm down until we get there!" At that point he looks at me and smiles and then gently rubs my arm. "Ahh, you're happy I came to visit?" He nods yes. "Yeah, me too Bubby. I'm so happy to see you." Somehow he has this amazing ability to make me completely forget my impatience, however temporarily.

Checking In

When we arrive at the office parking lot, I say to Jon, "You stay here and I'll be right back. Don't go anywhere, and no spitting!" He slaps his chest and points to the cabin we stayed in last time. "I'll be right back, Bubby, I have to get the key first." He slaps his chest again and points to the cabin. By this time I'm sweating from the heat. I've got to check in. "I'll be right back Bubby, I promise!" I go to the office and check in and get our keys, come back to the truck, and drive across the parking lot to our cabin; only this time it's a different cabin than the last time.

Again Jon points to the other cabin. "No, this time, we're in this cabin, Bubby. Now hush and come on!" I say it in a joking way, and he usually smiles, but still I'm impatient. I help him out of the truck. He points to the other cabin. "No, Jon, we're going here!" I say brusquely. I don't realize until later that he probably thinks I live there. When I lived in LA, he never visited. And now we live on the third floor of a one-bedroom apartment with no elevator or extra room for him to sleep in. I've always just come to him.

Anyway, he holds my hand as we walk slowly to the door of the cabin. I try the key and it doesn't work. Jon points. He wants the door open now. Jon only understands "now."

"The key doesn't work, Bubby. We've got to go back to the office and get a key that works. Come on." I take his hand and attempt to walk back to the truck and Jon stops. He's not moving, no matter what. "Jon, I've got to go back to the office to get a new key." Then he gives me the sign that he needs to go potty. Oh no. There's no way I'm going to get him into the truck and drive back to the office and back here in time. And he's not running. I've never left him alone like this, but I make the calculated decision to run for it. "Now Jon, stay right here. Don't you go anywhere! I mean anywhere. You stay right here. You promise?" He gives me the nod, yes.

So I tear across the field to the office and exchange the key. I run back and Jon hasn't moved, not an inch. Completely out of breath, I frantically open the door. "Good, Bubby, you did so good." Jon walks in and heads straight for the bathroom. It's a cute little one-room cabin, with a gas log fireplace, a small fridge, and a single bed for him and a king bed for me. He prefers the small bed. I walk into the bathroom and help him take down his pants, making sure the underpants clear the toilet. "Great, Bubby, we made it in time." No accidents. "You did good. Call me when you're done."

Finally! I get a minute to lie down on the bed. I'm exhausted; need to regroup. I take a breath in, and then let out a big exhale. Just when I'm almost relaxed, I hear a loud "SLAP, SLAP!"

The Bath

I get up out of bed and walk to the bathroom. He's butt naked on the toilet and points to the bathtub. "Oh, you're ready for a bath?" He nods. "Okay." I start a bath. Then he holds his arm out and makes a grasping motion with his hand. "The Epsom salts, okay." He nods. "I'll be right back." I have to go to the car and get a box of Epsom salts and my bag with the essential lavender oil in it.

As I walk out the door, I notice a woman sitting on the porch swing in front of the cabin next door. She smiles. I quickly go to the car to get the Epsom salts. Jon's waiting on me and the bath water is running. As I open the door, the woman asks, "Is that your brother with you?" "Yes," I say with a smile. Maybe she recognizes him from the film. "SLAP, SLAP!" "Ooops, I better go!" I wave the woman a friendly goodbye and walk in and pour some Epsom salts into Jon's bath. Then he holds his arm out and makes a pecking motion with his hand. I playfully yell at him, "I'm putting in the lavender oil, don't you worry!" He laughs. I shake a couple of drops of the lavender essential oil into the tub. Now the tub's full.

I turn off both spigots, dip my hand in the water, and swirl it around, giving the Epsom salts a chance to dissolve. Now Jon's ready to get in. Then I hold his hand as he steps over the ledge and gets into the tub.

Ahhh, he lets out a big exhale—perfect temperature. "That good, Bubby?" He nods. "Alright, lie down and I'll be back," thinking I can go lie down now. "SLAP, SLAP!" "What?" He does a pouring motion with his arm. "Oh, you want a pourer?" He nods. "Okay, I'll be right back."

I look around the cabin for anything resembling a big container. Those small drinking cups aren't big enough. His favorite at home is the Day's Inn ice bucket that Mom and Dad got for him somewhere in their travels. This container has to be at least that big, but the ice bucket here has a leather exterior. That won't work. I see a plastic liter water bottle that's almost empty. With my car keys I stab the water bottle, putting a hole in the side of it. Then I kind of saw off the top of the water bottle, making the perfect sized container. I hear the bathtub water on again. I walk back in. "Okay, Bubby, here you go, here's your pourer."

He takes the sawed-off water bottle and starts filling it from the spigot and pouring it into the tub. Filling and pouring. Filling and pouring. By now the tub is almost brimming with water. "That's it, Bubby, that's all you get! No more!" I turn off the spigot. "Now lie down and soak." He lies down. I start to walk out and when I'm just about out the door, "SLAP, SLAP!" "What?" He holds out the water bottle. "Okay!" For Jon, taking a bath is not a solo activity. Not because he can't do it alone, but because he prefers to be doted on. He lies down in the hot water and I dip the water bottle in the tub and pour it onto his back, over and over again.

Sometimes I get bored with the same activity over and over again. Then I remember that taking a bath is one of Jon's favorite activities. It's either this or something else. So since it makes him happy, I try to relax and continue pouring. He'd probably stay there as long as I was willing to refill the tub with hot water and pour.

I'm really tired after driving; I just want to lie down a little before we go out to dinner. "Alright, Bubby, that's it. Ready to get out?" I put the water bottle down and he's willing to get out. Great, maybe I can set him up with the TV and take a little nap, I hope.

Jon steps out of the tub and points to the towels and then to his head, letting me know he wants me to dry his hair. "Okay, okay." He sits on the toilet while I dry his hair and then his whole body. I hand him his underwear and he puts it on. Then he puts his Mickey Mouse t-shirt back on and is so happy he shakes his head and gives me a little happy dance. "Bubby's happy now, huh!?" He gives me the nod and smiles and walks out into the room and "SLAP, SLAP."

Getting Everything Just Right

He motions to the carpet. "Oh, you want me to move the carpet?" Yes, he nods. He wants me to move it from the middle of the room to alongside the fireplace where he likes to sit. "Okay, okay, Bubby." I get the rug situated just right and he sits on top of it and then, "SLAP, SLAP!" "WHAT!" He pats the rug. He points to the TV and does a little "come here" motion with his hand. "Oh, you want me to put the TV on the floor on the rug." He gives a double nod yes. "Okay!" I lift the TV off the dresser and bring it to the floor, turn it on, and give him the remote. I jokingly give him a hard time. "Are you happy now? Is everything absolutely perfect enough for you?!" He laughs. I finally go over to the bed to lie down. Ahhhh, I breathe. He'll be set for a little while now.

Just when I start to relax, "SLAP, SLAP." "What?!!" He puts his palms down and slides his hands outward, which is his sign for folding paper. "You want some foldin'?" Yes, he nods. "Okaaaaaaay, this is it!" I get up and get him some paper. He points at it, wanting me to separate each sheet. "Okay, okay!" I quickly create a pretty good stack of paper, sheet by sheet. "There you go! Now that's it! I'm going to rest now, okay? I don't want to hear another word from you!" He laughs.

Let the Folding Begin!

Great, he loves folding paper. And I'm exhausted. It feels incredible to lie down. I lie on my side watching Jon. "I'm going to rest just a little bit, okay, Bubby?" He nods yes and rolls a piece of paper up his stomach, then folds it over his nose and then throws it across the room. I close my eyes and begin to doze off. There's a certain rhythmic sound of the clicking of the paper as he rolls it up his belly, the click of the fold over the nose, and then the thump of the throw landing. Click, click, click, and then thump. Click, click, click, thump. It's one of those sounds that feels so familiar and comforting to me. It's the sound that all is well with Bubby. I can relax. I fall asleep for a moment. One of those quick ten-minute deep sleeps.

All of a sudden I am awakened by a folded paper hitting me. "Jon!" He laughs and slaps his chest. "What?" He gives me the sign for more paper. "Okay!" I begrudgingly get up and separate an even larger stack of paper, sheet by sheet, into a big pile in front of him. "Now hush!" I go back to bed, close my eyes, and try to sleep some more.

Multiply this scenario by ten and you have a pretty good idea of our next hour. With the TV on in the background, the click, click, click, thump. Click, click, click, thump. Then a fold hits me. Then it's time to get up and separate more folding. Then back to bed. Click, click, click, thump. Click, click, click thump. And so it goes until I hear a big "SLAP, SLAP!" "What, Jon?" This time he points to his mouth. "You hungry?" He nods yes.

Dinner

"Alright, let's get your pants on." Jon slowly walks over to his bed and sits and puts his pants on. Nothing happens too fast with Jon. Then I hand him his Velcro-fastened tennis shoes and he puts them on. Then he motions for me to fix them. He's already fastened them; he just wants me to do it three times each. Rip, fasten, rip, fasten, rip, fasten. Then the other shoe. Rip, fasten, rip, fasten, rip, fasten. Okay, now he's ready to walk out the door. "SLAP, SLAP!" Jon points to his new ears. They must go to dinner with us. "Okay, Bubby, I got 'em. Let's go get some spaghetti!" He nods. He loves spaghetti.

I hold his hand as he slowly walks down the two steps and I try to walk him toward the passenger side of the car, but he's not moving. "Bubby, we've got to get in the truck to go to the restaurant." He nods no. "Are you hungry?" He nods yes. "Well, we have to get in the truck to go!" Nope, he's not budging. I suppose this could be his idea of an argument. Then he points to his wheelchair. "Okay, okay, I'll wheel you to the car!" I get his wheelchair out and wheel it over to him. He sits in it and then points to the onsite restaurant where we get our breakfast buffet in the mornings. "No, Bubby, we're going in the truck to another restaurant to get your spaghetti." He grunts defiantly and points toward the onsite restaurant with a huff. "Oh, you want to eat there." Yes, he nods. The breakfast buffet is one thing, but for lunch and dinner the onsite restaurant is a four star restaurant. But once he's decided, he's decided. So I guess we'll see how this goes.

I wheel him into the restaurant. The hostess kindly seats us in a room with two other occupied tables. It's very quiet with classical music playing in the background. At one table a formally dressed, gray-haired couple is almost finished with dinner. The other table appears to be a small dinner party with three couples, probably in their late fifties. I don't ever remembering being so aware of how quiet it is until Jon starts honking and grunting in displeasure at the tablecloth hanging down. "Okay, Bubby, calm down! I'll fix it," I say under my breath. I take the tablecloth and fold it under, in between the table and the tablecloth on top. It doesn't look great, but Jon's happy with it. Great, I think, we're going to get through this.

Right then, the waitress comes to the table with menus. She notices the tablecloth; looks at Jon. There's always that moment of recognition and readjustment. Clearly Jon is different, though she pretends not to notice as she hands us each a menu. "Just one menu is fine." She turns around to get some water. She's obviously uncomfortable. If she only knew how uncomfortable I am! "Now Bubby, have good manners!" He lets out a mild roar of acknowledgement. She walks over assuming he's ready to order. I quickly order the ravioli special for him and the lamb for me, and a glass of red wine. Lord, I need it!

The waitress turns around and walks over to the gray-haired couple. I overhear her asking about their dinner. "And how was your steak?" The gentleman dressed in a coat and tie answers with an air of arrogance, "The steak was just a bit overcooked, more medium than medium-rare as I had ordered, but the rest of the meal was superb." Right at that moment Jon burps very loudly. "Excuse me!" I take one for the team. Completely unaffected, Jon puts on his earphones and yawns loudly. His noises become even more profound in the silence.

I sip my red wine, watching Jon as he changes the channel on his "ears." I overhear a matronly woman at the table across the room telling the other couples about growing up on an orange orchard and the wonderful cakes their live-in maid, Miss Melissa, made for her as a child. I remember thinking how different her life was from mine growing up. And at the same time thinking how common this experience is when I am out to dinner with Jon—listening to other people's conversations and making up stories of their lives in my mind while he sits there in his own world listening to his earphones.

The waitress comes back with our dinners. Jon takes off his earphones. His ravioli is very fancy with julienne vegetables and no red sauce. It isn't Chef Boyardee; I hope he likes it. He makes a slicing motion with his hands. "You want me to cut it up?" Yes, he nods. I cut up his ravioli and he starts eating. I have a bite of my lamb. I want to have a conversation with Jon, connect with him. "Are you happy, Bubby?" He nods yes. "Are you liking your new workshop?" Yes, he nods and takes another bite of ravioli. "How about staying at Sandra's—do you like it there?" Again, he nods yes. That's pretty much the whole conversation for the night. I eat my lamb. And wonder. I hope he's happy. He seems happy. Then he burps again. Back to reality.

The waitress comes back and asks how our dinner was. "Great, thanks." A nice formality but the truth is I'm just trying to get out of here without a loud fart. "You're doing real good, Bubby." Jon puts both hands up to the side of his face, motioning that he's tired. "You ready to go to bed, Bubby?" He nods yes. We finish our dinner and I wheel him back to the room.

Bedtime

We come back to the cabin. Jon takes off his pants and shoes and lies down on his bed. "SLAP, SLAP!" He rubs his arm, which is the sign for his Furby. I bring him his lunchbox. He pulls out the Furby and rubs it against his cheek. He loves his Furby up and places it on the chair beside his bed. He pulls out his Wuv Luv and loves him up and places him beside the Furby on the chair. Then he pulls out his new comb and scratches his belly with it and places it beside his Wuv Luv. "SLAP, SLAP!" He points to his head. "Oh, you want your ears. Okay." I get his new ears from the back of the wheelchair and bring them to him. He places them in line beside his Wuv Luv. Now he's officially ready for bed.

I lean down and kiss and hug him goodnight. "I love you, Bubby. You're my absolute favorite in the whole wide world." He gives me the "I love you" sign. There is a part of me that wants just a little bit more. I walk over to my bed and finally lie down. Jon makes a clicking noise and another. Many think that because Jon doesn't talk, spending time with him is very quiet. Wrong. There are so many different noises that he makes. Some I'm still becoming familiar with. I stay quiet and try to go to sleep. Then he kicks off his covers and sits up. "What is it, Bubby?" I turn on the light. He lies back down, his head is where his feet should go, watching me. "Okay, I'm going to go to sleep now, Bubby." He nods yes. "Now you go to sleep too, Bubby." He nods again. "Well, turn around and go to bed, Bubby!" He growls and laughs. "Oh, you just want to watch me?" Yes, he nods. "Okay, I'm going to sleep now. I'm going to turn out the light." He nods. I turn out the light and go to sleep.

Later that night I wake up to use the bathroom. I check on Jon. I cover him with a soft blanket. He reaches up and pulls me down and loves me up like he does his Furby, messing up my hair and gently bouncing his head against mine for a good several minutes. Then he kisses me. Wow. That was worth everything. I am complete.

The next morning as I carry my bags out to the truck, the woman from next door looks over and said, "You're a saint." If she only knew. If anyone's a saint, it's Sandra. I've only been with Jon for the last twenty-four hours and I'm exhausted. Sandra does this every day. All I know is that after being with Jon and dealing with his Furby and ears and folding paper, it's given me a whole new perspective on the feng shui and rooflines. My priorities are now in order and I can't wait to come back and visit my Bubby again.

* * *

*After working as a personal assistant to actors on twenty-five feature films, **Jennifer Owensby** left Hollywood to produce and direct her* *first film,* The Teachings of Jon, *which is currently airing nationally on public television. Winning the coveted 2007 Silver Telly Award,* The Teachings of Jon *has been praised across the country as the "family feel good film of the year." Passionate about holistic health, living sustainably, and evolving spiritually, Jennifer currently lives with her husband in Hillsborough, North Carolina, and travels internationally raising consciousness about changing perceptions of people with mental disabilities.*

19.
Willingness to Change

Nancy Werlin

I've flown home from Baltimore on Christmas Eve day, even though I was invited to stay with my boyfriend and his family through Christmas. As soon as my plane lands, I head for my sister's apartment to pick her up. She'll be staying with me for several days. This has been our tradition (even though we are Jewish, we require a Christmas tradition). It is important to me to make sure my sister has holiday plans. Plans, presents, family. We have other family members, but I am the main one for her. I am "it," and I have been for many years, and I expect always to be.

She seems happy and untroubled when I pick her up. This is a relief, because when I told her I was going away for the weekend before Christmas, she asked, "Can I come?"

"No, not this time," I said. "I'm going to visit Jim's family. But you'll have a chance to meet them later on, I promise. And I'll be home to get you on Christmas Eve, and we'll spend Christmas together as we always do. I've already made our reservation for the brunch at the Seaport Hotel."

I was rattled. It was hard for me to say this "no" to my sister, and indeed, only possible for me to allow myself to visit my boyfriend's family at all because I'd made the plan to come back before Christmas. Only later did I realize that my sister's desire to come with me to Baltimore was unlikely to be about her wanting to meet Jim's family, but about wanting to travel, which she loves to do.

We are on the verge of huge change, my sister and I. I am forty-six years old. I never thought I would marry and didn't think I wished to. But now, to my astonishment and very great happiness, this has changed.

But with the change comes anxiety and fear. How do I reassure my sister? How will she adjust to change? How will I? We were the single daughters. Despite our differences, we were a pair. There was reassurance in that, and safety, and routine, for both of us.

In telling her the Christmas plans, I had carefully avoided talking to her about New Year's Eve. This, too, we have often, if not always, spent together. But soon after I pick her up, she asks me.

"I'm going away over New Year's with Jim," I say. I take a deep breath, and then I add: "Jim and I are courting. When a couple are courting, that means they're thinking seriously about marriage. During a courtship, they need to spend time alone together, and that's what we're doing. We are probably going to be married. So, I can't be with you on New Year's Eve."

"Oh," my sister says, and then adds, "Very interesting."

There is no explosion or difficulty. She seems pragmatic. I explain further that, in marrying, I would still live where I do now, and would not move away to another state, as our other sister did.

A few days later, my sister pulls together a little Christmas present for Jim—a (slightly used) bottle of aspirin, which is a very typical present-type from my sister. This delights me, and Jim, who is beginning to get to know her, and who says, when I tell him this story, "Well, it *is* very interesting."

What the future will hold, I don't exactly know. Plans, presents, family. These are now happening for me with someone else. There will always be a place in my life for my sister, but it won't be the same. Things will change, that's all I know and all I can know. That, and the fact that I will always be nearby. In choosing a husband, I am not changing my choice to be "it" for my sister.

But I will be a different "it," all the same. It scares me, because the "it" that I was worked very well.

My sister is the one with autism, supposedly the one who wants things to be always the same. But I think it may have taken me all of these forty-six years to find my own willingness to change, willingness to open my life and my heart fully.

* * *

Nancy Werlin *is the author of six young-adult novels, including* The Rules of Survival, *which was a 2006 National Book Award finalist, and* The Killer's Cousin, *which won the Edgar award for best young adult mystery in 1999. Her first novel,* Are You Alone on Purpose?, *was about a teenage girl with an autistic twin brother.* Impossible, *Nancy's seventh novel, was published in September, 2008. She lives near Boston, Massachusetts, and you can visit her web site at www.nancywerlin.com.*

20.
The Call

Daniel Mont

The phone rings and I glance at the caller ID screen. In neat little letters I see my sister's name, and immediately a flurry of conflicting emotions career inside my head. Nothing unpredictable. Of course not. They are the same flurry of emotions as always, because they lie lurking, preparing for the next time they are called to action.

What are these emotions? Fear, because I never know when a calamitous situation will develop that I will be called upon to diffuse. Anger, because there are a host of unresolved issues from my childhood that I still see with child's eyes—pain and stress and lost opportunities. Sadness—because my sister really does try so hard and has had so many aching moments. Shame, because being an adult and knowing what I know about my sister, why can't I move beyond that anger? Frustration, because our conversations are like something from Kafka or Sartre, a never-ending loop that seems impossible to break—a bizarre funhouse of mirrors designed to cast the same reflection no matter how you try to escape. But there is also hope, a little ray of hope that maybe this time we will have a "normal" brother and sister conversation, that I will enjoy talking with her, that I'll have an opportunity to feel my love for her more than all that fear, anger, sadness, frustration, and shame.

This cocktail of emotions is always the same. It is instantaneous and powerful, but I have to admit that over the years my little ray of hope is getting rewarded more often than in the past. When my sister was in her twenties, her life was a cyclone that sucked all of us up in its path—police, institutions, public outbursts, and altercations. She is over forty now, much more stable, almost content, calmer, and nearly independent. If my parents could see her now, they would rest much easier in their graves knowing the woman she has become and the life she has built for herself.

But when that phone rings....a lifetime shoots across my chest. Just for an instant. And my friends who know me as a patient, understanding, relatively unflappable guy would be shocked to see how quickly I can become agitated and practically start yelling into the phone. I've seen my children looking at me, wondering what's going on and why their aunt can bring out this dark side in their father at the drop of a hat. But how can I explain a lifetime of stress, fights, disappointment, frustrations, and fears? It took my wife many years of marriage to truly get a handle on our relationship.

I'll always be there for my sister. I'm her surrogate father now. And my other sister is her surrogate mom. It's the three of us now, and while we live in separate homes, we are still family.

But my sister's issues are complex. I have a hard time sorting out where her learning disabilities end and her emotional problems begin. What is mental illness, what is manipulation, and what portion of her incredible gaps in knowledge and norms are due to the formative years she missed out on because she was consumed by other things? And, what used to disturb me most, what part of her behavior results from being pampered because she was the youngest child and so physically and emotionally exhausting for my parents? These things used to bother me more. I'm better at accepting her as she is regardless of the "why" and prioritizing what's important. Not perfect by any means, but better.

When I was a teenager, though, I had many criticisms of my parents. I thought they didn't expect enough of her, and I told them so. So it was quite a jolt when my son Simon said to me, "Dad, you're too easy on Alex."

You see, my oldest son, Alex, has autism. He is unlike my sister in so many ways, but my parents and I did have a lot in common: exhaustion, self-doubts as to whether we were doing the best we could, and the concern over letting the problems of one child crowd out the problems of the others.

"You let him get away with murder," says Simon. I know exactly how he feels. In fact, being my sister's brother has given me the blessing of being a better father to Simon. At least I hope it has. I know it has enabled me to understand him better. I, too, had moments of embarrassment at how my sister acted in public. I had moments of disappointment when the family couldn't do certain things, or when I couldn't have the sibling relationship of which I dreamed. And, I had moments of fiercely coming to her defense when the outside world attacked, while at the same time harboring resentments when inside the confines of my home.

"You think I let him get away with stuff?" I asked. Was I being too easy on Alex in order to be easy on myself? Was I being too soft because I knew how hard certain situations could be for him?

"Yeah, he can sit at the table in a restaurant and not walk around making all those noises."

I didn't think so. And even if he could, was that really what we wanted to spend our energy on? We couldn't work on all of Alex's behaviors at once. We had to pick our battles. Be strategic. Otherwise it would be too much for him and he could totally shut down or rebel. And besides, the goal was to help him get through life, not straitjacket him into behaving exactly like a non-autistic person. That, in my opinion, is both inappropriate and unfair.

I'm a smart guy. I could easily rationalize all of Simon's feelings away. But I remember my own…heck, I feel my own…too strongly to do that. The truth, as always, is probably in the middle somewhere. And the last thing I want to do is brush Simon's feelings aside.

He's going to carry them for the rest of his life, and they are going to color his relationship with Alex for a good while.

Their relationship. That pains me. Little in this world would make me happier than to see my two sons have a close brotherly relationship. But their relationship will be far from typical. Oh, they love each other. I can see that they'll always be able to rely on each other. But their ways of being in a relationship are so fundamentally different.

Twenty years from now, Simon is going to look at a phone and wonder whether he should call Alex. Alex won't call him much. That just isn't who Alex is. Will Simon make that call? Out of obligation, like I do? With a little ray of hope that he will have a genuine conversation with his brother? Will images of me and my wife pop into his head the way my parents hover around me whenever I pick up the phone? Will he forgive me for my missteps as I have learned to forgive them for theirs?

* * *

Daniel Mont *lives in the Washington, D.C. area and is a Senior Economist with The World Bank's Disability and Development Team, helping to make economic development projects in poor countries more inclusive. He originally joined the Bank as a Joseph P. Kennedy Foundation Public Policy Fellow in 2002. He is also the author of* A Different Kind of Boy: A Father's Memoir about Raising a Gifted Child with Autism. *While not working, he performs with Precipice Improvisational Theater and has had a number of plays produced in the D.C. area, New York City, and Baltimore. He and his wife are now empty nesters with two boys in college, missing them but enjoying the freedom.*

21.
Happy Ending, Complicated Beginning

Sherry Gray

My sister Suzy and I watched the movie *Rain Man* for the first time recently. At the end Suzy whooped with joy when Raymond Babbitt got on the train and his brother Charlie promised to see him soon. For Suzy, trains symbolize happiness because three years ago she moved from Indianapolis to Saint Paul, Minnesota, on Amtrak's Empire Builder. It was the grandest adventure of her life and her very best memory.

Moving to Minnesota meant that Suzy got a family who was actively involved in her life for the first time since she was three years old. It meant seeing my husband, David, and me every few days, instead of every three months. She knew what a train had meant to her and what it would mean for Raymond: A good life where your sibling takes care of you after many years living alone and unloved in institutions.

While Suzy expressed her joy at Raymond's good fortune, I watched Charlie and saw affection and exasperation flicker over his face in that final scene. Charlie had only recently discovered the existence of his older brother, Raymond, a man diagnosed with autism who lived in a secluded institution. I knew that Charlie Babbitt would soon undertake a new journey, the same one I did three years ago. Charlie and I had ended up in the same place from an earlier journey, both of us having fallen in love with our sibling and both of us at a train station committing ourselves to our sibling's care forever. I could tell that Charlie was just learning how Raymond was quietly taking control of his life, just as Suzy has quietly taken control of mine.

Rain Man is a classic American road trip film and like all films in this genre, the trip always involves both physical travel and emotional growth. Watching the Babbitt brothers' journey, I observed how the tiny demands of Raymond's ostensibly simple life one by one derailed the routines, even meanings, of Charlie's life until Charlie appeared helpless in the face of his strong-willed—yet undeniably vulnerable—brother. Raymond's life was transformed too as Charlie introduced him to the colorful and chaotic society that existed outside the unchanging rhythms of his institution.

Unlike Charlie, I always knew I had a sister, but what I thought I knew about her proved to be wrong. I thought my sister was a "vegetable" as our father once wrote about her and that the sum of her intelligence and personality was "nothing there but a sweet little smile," as our mother wrote.

Our family believed that Suzy could not know us, had no memory, and would not live to adulthood. We told each other that she had no personality, contradicting our memories from her baby years at home that she had a wicked sense of humor and easily demonstrated what she liked and disliked. We believed this even though on our visits to her in the early years after she left home she called out our names. And we believed she would soon die, even though by 1998 she'd lived thirty-seven years, thirty-four of them in institutions.

In 1998 I went looking for my sister and thanks to a perceptive and kind social worker, I learned that Suzy was healthy, smart, had a strong personality, and needed me. David and I became Suzy's co-guardians a year later and began a journey together that has changed all our lives. Suzy gained a real family for the first time since she was a toddler and David and I gained a charming but strong-willed dependent. With Suzy we took on legal responsibility for another person for the first time since we married. "It was the right thing to do," said David then, neither of us ever questioning that decision since.

In 2004 a specialist in disability issues recommended that we move my sister to Minnesota in order to more closely monitor and advocate for better care for her. The process moved fast in both states, and seven months later Suzy and I were sitting on the train heading for Saint Paul.

She was excited, even ecstatic, to leave her dull, ugly institution and find a new life in the bigger world. I was excited and apprehensive at the responsibility we'd undertaken. The night she arrived and was settled into a hotel near Mall of America, David smiled at me and said, "You did it. You got her here." I felt exulted and terrified, a mix of strong, contradictory feelings that I hadn't felt since the day David and I married, me standing at the altar crying tears of joy and fear.

Three years later, my sister lives in a comfortable, newly built group home located on a quiet street in a leafy small town not far from us. Her room is painted brilliant yellow (her choice) and decorated with photos of our family and her life's events. She attends a fun and challenging day program, goes swimming, has joined a local church, and is a regular at her community's friendly diner. She volunteers monthly at a day care center and goes out frequently to activities and events. We keep her busy and surrounded by love.

But making this situation possible for Suzy takes a great deal of my time. The demands of her care mean that everything we do is in partnership with the Suzy Team: Direct care staff, institutional administrators, medical professionals, legal and financial advisors, and the county case manager. We coordinate activities and share our lives with Suzy's housemates and their families. Working with so many different people and institutions means that many days I am operating as the communications director, keeping everyone informed and on schedule. Some days I take on other roles, including conflict resolution specialist, staff trainer, or guerrilla fighter.

I don't make things easy for myself, often adding new items to my already long to-do list for Suzy. Determined to give my sister the best life possible, to erase forty years of institutional carelessness, and to rewrite this unhappy family history into a story of love, I fuss over every detail of Suzy's life. I decorate her room, organize her clothes into matching outfits, and carefully read all her reports and documents. I attend her medical and therapy appointments, keep detailed records about her, and push organizations to provide opportunities for Suzy to participate in the community, go swimming, get range-of-motion exercises, and be well-groomed. In the past three years I have rearranged my weekly schedule around my sister, going to church (which I hate) with her (which she loves), taking her swimming Thursday nights, watching movies together every Sunday night, and hanging with her many Saturday mornings. In organizing my activities around her needs, I have assumed that my life is more flexible than hers.

Now I need to find my life again. I've transmuted from a globetrotting careerist to a homebody life manager for my sister. I spend part of nearly every day doing something for Suzy. Her friends are now my friends. I quit working and now volunteer in my community on projects to support my sister, her nonprofit service providers, and our larger disability community. Some days I worry about losing myself, about becoming my sister's assistant instead of living my own life. And sometimes I get angry at my sister, especially on those days when I think she's being stubborn or selfish. On those days I feel that she has more power in our relationship.

But most days I just love my sister and feel grateful that we found each other. Suzy has taught me about the core elements of being human—elements not dependent on the ability to walk or talk—including the universal human need for love and for others to assist us in attaining our life goals. I admire Suzy for her lack of inhibition about her body or embarrassment over its function, for her strong sense of self, and for her phenomenal survival skills. She lives vibrantly despite her physical limitations, her dependence upon others, and her inability to care or provide for herself.

I feel the power that comes to me from my sister's joyfulness in life, the metamorphosis I have undergone in joining a community that admits disabilities easily, and the expansiveness of making friends with people whose notions of human life are a radical and happy change from the society of perfection-seeking, sometimes narcissistic, people I have known most of my life.

I feel the power of the message that people like my charming and determined sister deserve to be seen in our communities, listened to, and loved. That to accept the humanity and rights of the most disabled among us is to accept the broadest, least discriminatory concept of ourselves and others.

In *Rain Man,* Charlie made the same life transition I have made. He began his journey with Raymond as a man self-sufficient financially and emotionally. He ended his journey recovering the love—and need for love—that he had buried deep in his heart as a child. Each brother discovered that he needed the other in this journey. At the film's end, Raymond gets his brother's help while Charlie recovers his family and his heart.

As I watched Charlie and Raymond, I thought about what strengths and weaknesses each of them would bring to their new relationship. For Suzy and me, our three years together as very small children and then the long years we lived in widely disparate circumstances left us with distinct strengths and weaknesses.

Suzy grew up pragmatic and a tough institutional fighter, quickly learning good girl/bad girl strategies to get attention to her needs. She learned that no one stays around long in her life and so when someone she likes tells her they are leaving, she turns away and refuses to make eye contact. When I see her do this self-protective tactic, I imagine that she's lost hundreds of kind caregivers over her forty-six years. When she reveals her anxiety that David and I will abandon her or never return from a vacation, I want to cry for this scar on her heart.

I grew up alternately disillusioned and idealistic. I lost trust in my family and felt keenly the injustice I saw in the world around me. I grew up fearful that if anything happened to me, I would be sent away too, and forgotten. But I also believed that our story could have unfolded differently and I never stopped believing that humans could choose love over hate, peace over war, and responsibility over abandonment. I believed humans could forge better societies and rework bad histories into better futures. I believed this about Suzy and me too.

Suzy enjoys movies full of action and angst but with happy endings for the main characters, so she was delighted and relieved to see Raymond was getting on the train and Charlie was making future plans. She identified with this story because it was like her own. I like movies that help us understand our human condition, so the portrayal of Charlie's emotional growth fascinated me. I identified with Charlie and saw not only a man who found a brother and filled a hole in his heart, but also a man uncertain about how he will manage this new life of responsibility and commitment. Where Suzy saw a happy ending, I saw a complicated beginning.

* * *

Sherry Gray was born in Indianapolis in 1960 and grew up in Colorado. She studied at the Universities of Colorado and Denver, earning a Ph.D. in international studies in 1992. When this essay was written, Sherry had taken a career sabbatical to oversee a transformation in her sister's care and to work on writing and volunteer projects; currently she works at the University of Minnesota. Sherry now lives in Saint Paul, Minnesota with her husband, David Blaney. David is a professor of political science at Macalester College and shares guardianship of Suzy. Suzy Gray was born in Indianapolis in 1961 and lived in Indiana institutions for forty years before moving to Minnesota. She has been diagnosed with cerebral palsy, mental retardation, kyphoscoliosis, and epilepsy. Suzy also has excellent eyesight and extraordinary peripheral vision, keen hearing, and a healthy sense of her own self-worth.

22.
A Break for Freedom

Tarri Lucier

I tap on my brother's bedroom door one Saturday morning and stick my head inside. "Hi, Vinny!" I say in my most cheerful tone. Vinny is sitting on his bed waiting for my weekly visit. "How are you doing, today?"

"Hanging on by fingernails!" he replies.

This has been his standard reply since he moved into this "level four" (fully supervised) home for adults with disabilities two months ago, but when I look at his grinning face I'm cheered. When Vinny says, *hanging on by fingernails,* he's giving me the good news: that he's recovering from our mother's death and all the changes that have happened since, and that he's not about to give up now.

It's a new life for Vincent in this quiet, suburban tract home. Prior to this, he had lived with our parents for the thirty-nine years of his life. Three months earlier our mother had passed away, leaving her husband, eleven children, twenty grandchildren, and four great-grandchildren bereft of her supportive presence. Besides her husband of forty-eight years, probably no one felt it more than Vincent. Since

I, his oldest sister, had moved back home two years ago to finish my college degree, I had gotten to know him better than I ever had before, and was a witness to his life there.

Our mother had cared for Vincent on a daily basis all of his life, cooking his meals, brushing his teeth, washing his hair, taking him to sports practice, and trying to keep him in a chipper, motivated routine with household chores and a coopful of chickens that needed his attention. But there was something missing in his life that she was helpless to fulfill—something that had caused him to quit his job and sports activities, and quietly withdraw from her and everyone else.

When I moved back into the family home, I did what I could to help Vinny out by stimulating his intellectual and creative capacities, like taking him to the movies and the library. In his teens, he'd enjoyed reading Hardy Boys and Nancy Drew mysteries, so I helped him check out the newest volumes. But after he'd read those, he seemed lost as to what to read next. So I introduced him to the wonders of the nonfiction section. With armloads of books on medieval history, travel, and biography, he spent many absorbed hours in his room. Somehow he came up with the idea of asking me to draw images from the books, which turned into a nightly practice of sitting in my room and listening to music while we collaborated on increasingly complex pieces of work.

At the same time, I saw that he was restless with his life. He spent most of his time in his room with the door shut, sleeping or watching TV late into the night. Other symptoms of his frustration included collecting newspapers, which piled up in closets, drawers, and under the bed, as well as his increasingly strained relationship with our mother. Where once he appreciated her pampering attention, now he grew defiant of her rules about showering, and had shouting matches with her over his right to leave the neighborhood and walk alone to the local 7-11, which she denied him for his own safety. There was a lot of tension in the house because of this. When our mother became ill, and then was diagnosed with pancreatic cancer, and then was hospitalized, something in Vinny saw her coming demise as a chance to make a break for freedom.

So one day, when no one was looking, he packed his bags and made his way toward the front door. Our dad tried to stop him, and that's when Vinny became violent. There was a confrontation and I was forced to call the police. To the whole family's distress, Vinny was placed in the lockdown ward of the county hospital. Because our dad had to be home with our mom, I stayed in the hospital to make sure Vinny was okay. The staff kindly gave us the visiting room, which had a TV and VCR, and we watched movies through the night, while agitated patients let off steam nearby.

What surprised me the most was Vinny's response when a loudly defiant patient would let loose. He laughed with glee.

"Why is that funny to you?" I asked.

"New experiences!" he said with a delighted chuckle.

Indeed, he seemed to be enjoying himself. The next day I watched him stand up for unhappy patients a number of times. He seemed to identify with their helplessness when the staff would administer control measures. I was glad I was there to talk to him, and to mediate and explain his idiosyncrasies to nurses who may have taken restraining measures against him for his attempts at intervention.

Due to policies about holding adults with disabilities, Vinny was released within twenty-four hours, but forty-eight hours later he was back in the hospital—this time at Kaiser, where he is a member—for another violent episode at home. It was so bizarre to me, this violence, as Vinny had always been the most peaceful and gentle of people as far back as I could remember. Was he doing this in order to change what had come to be an intolerable situation to him?

As our mother quickly slipped away from this earth, I did my best to find a solution for Vincent's dilemma of where to live. Working with an organization known simply as "Regional," I spent hours on the phone, pacing the hospital hallways, and checking in on my brother who was sitting, bored, in a hospital bed, watched by a security guard. In those days at Kaiser, I began to understand Vinny's tactics. I realized, as I saw him tease the guard, and make pretend lunges at him and then laugh, that he was purposefully going through this in order to be independent. He was making his own mistakes without Mom overseeing him. He was growing up.

I finally made a connection with a board and care facility for adults who require "level four" care. It was a brand new facility, and Vincent was the first client to be interviewed. A kindly Philippine gentleman arrived at the hospital for the appointment, and spent forty-five minutes talking to Vincent and me. I was impressed with his respectful attitude toward my brother. He said he had just acquired the license, which took two years to obtain, and he had worked for many years in a local state hospital with developmentally disabled adults, and was a minister besides. His plan was to provide a home where disadvantaged individuals would feel respected and validated for who they were. The name of the home was *Dreams Come True*, and I prayed that it would live up to its title.

Vincent was excited to move into his new home, and I had packed his bags, including his Scooby Doo bedspread, his hundreds of videos, and his favorite t-shirts and sweatshirts. He had his pick of the four bedrooms, chose one of the two single-occupant rooms, and began to settle in. Over the next several weeks, I visited a number of times and was touched to see the care that Mark, his caregiver, had provided in hanging and displaying items for Vinny, whose characteristic zaniness was blossoming, complete with Looney Tunes stuffed animals hanging from the ceiling by strings, and swimsuit models (which had not been allowed in our parents' home) taped to the wall next to his bed.

New housemates were slow in coming, and didn't remain very long, and Vinny grew lonely as he eagerly anticipated the house filling up with friends. However, his relationship with Mark was excellent. And still is. Mark has become genuinely fond of Vincent, and impressed with his level of wit and intelligence.

A year has passed since Vinny informed me that he was "hanging on by fingernails." Things have changed a lot. In that year, he has matured rapidly. Because he's had the freedom to make his own choices and to interact with someone entirely outside of our close family circle, he has grown up beyond what we ever expected. His relationship with our dad has healed, he chats often with his siblings on the phone, and he lunches with one or the other when time permits. Plus, he's more independent than ever and can look forward to the future, knowing that things can change. And for that, my siblings and I are forever grateful.

* * *

Tarri Lucier *has been a working artist for twenty years, and recently graduated with a bachelor's degree with honors in the Practice of Art from U.C. Berkeley. Her family is a primary source of inspiration for works of art, whether it is her immediate family of parents and ten siblings, or her own four children and four grandchildren. She lives and exhibits in the San Francisco Bay Area. Tarri's sister, Veronica Chater, is the author of "Walkout" (p. 86).*

23.
Riding to the Fountain with My Sister

Rachel Simon

My sister Beth is already waiting for me when I enter the bus center. *Of course* she's already here—the bus center is where I always meet her, and she's always on time, eager to chide me if I'm one minute late. That's something I've learned about my forty-seven-year-old sister over the past several years: despite not wearing a watch or having a job, she times everything to the second. She does this because she lives on bus time, speeding down sidewalks from one stop to the next, her entire existence, for twelve hours every day, orchestrated around bus schedules.

I love my sister, and I've even learned to love buses, drivers, and her bus riding lifestyle. But I don't share her zippy pace. I, eleven months older, prefer writer time, which means the kind of contemplative, lose-track-of-time pace I need to write books. This presents a problem, because even when I try my hardest, such as I did this morning, leaving early for my two-hour drive to her city, I'm rarely able to satisfy her insistence on precision. I'll need to stop for a bathroom, or I'll hit traffic. Sometimes both of us will take it in stride when this happens, but sometimes her annoyance, or my feelings of guilt, will taint the whole visit. When that happens, I'll ask myself if I'll ever really master how to balance her desires with my needs. I've made a lot of progress with the emotional side of our visits since I've come to embrace her buses. But today, after almost fifty years of history with each other, I still wonder, as I see her standing at an empty bus stop a few lanes away, how can I be a "good sister" while also respecting myself? How can I answer that question once and for all?

Fortunately, I can shelve these thoughts now, because it's only 12:17 p.m., which means I got here with three whole minutes of leeway. Not that Beth appears to know this yet. As the doors to the bus center close behind me, I see her more clearly across the lanes, dressed in Barney-purple coat and pants, and I put up my hand to say hello. But even though she's turned toward me, she doesn't wave back or smile my way. Her vision has weakened over the years, and her vanity still rejects the idea of glasses, so it's reasonable to conclude that she simply can't see this far across the bus center. At the same time, I wonder, as I do whenever she shows no excitement at my arrival, if she's actually taking me for granted, or is stuck between wanting and resenting me, or sees me as too inconsequential to deserve visual acknowledgment.

But today is supposed to be a celebratory day, so I force myself not to think that. This isn't hard—my mind has always bounced from one question to another when I'm with Beth, and now, feeling a surge of love as I watch her, a lone figure shifting her weight in the chill air, craning her neck as she waits for driver Jacob to appear, it's easy for me to give myself only positive answers. After all, for years she wrote letters saying she loves me. Although the letters have mostly stopped, she still gives me homemade cards at every visit that say the same. She must love me, even if she doesn't express love in the exact way I want her to. And she must know I love her. I visit often. Her friends have become my friends. We even planned today together, and I made it here with three—now two—minutes to spare. When Jacob pulls in at 12:20 for his lunch break and she springs his birthday celebration on him, I'll already be standing beside her, our secret gift to make the ensuing festivities even merrier.

I could call out hello to let her know I'm here, but now her back is to me, and anyway, the bus lane I'm crossing reverberates with the roar of engines. So I just make my way toward my sister, passing through hundreds, thousands, decades of memories, from our baths together when we were toddlers, where my body helped her sustain a seated position, to her medical appointment last month, where my presence helped her stop shoving the poor physician away.

I remember the sweep of time, too: the many years, when I was a kid and adolescent, when people asked me almost nothing about her, nor about our relationship. It seemed as if it was enough for them to know that I had a sister with a disability, the one then called mental retardation. They might go as far as to ask if she had Down syndrome, to which I would say no, and sometimes I'd add that there was no known reason for her disability. Then they might venture to ask me her "mental age" or her I.Q. But I wanted to protect my sister, with her spunky, stubborn, colorful, complicated personality, from such limited, and limiting, notions—as well as from questions I saw as unanswerable or rude. So I'd say, truthfully, that I didn't know, but add, "What's *your* mental age? *Your* I.Q.? What are *mine*?" And that would be the end of the conversation.

I softened when we reached adulthood, but the lack of curiosity from others did not waver. It was those same shallow questions, over and over. Never anything about what TV shows Beth liked and I didn't, or what names—nice and nasty—we called each other. Never anything about how it felt to have a sister who inspired waitresses to ask me, "What does she want to order?" This apparent disinterest prompted me to ponder different kinds of questions than I asked myself in her company, but they were questions all the same. Were people just afraid to find out more about her? Did they imagine her diagnosis was all that mattered? Were they so certain that my life must be so rich with blessings, or so crammed with responsibilities, that I was simply too saintly to be subjected to further inquiry? Eventually I did answer myself, though that didn't happen for years.

Until then, I sometimes pressed the issue and offered information they hadn't requested. In our late twenties, I said that she'd moved into a group home; in our mid-thirties, that she was now in her own apartment. Still, no one followed up. No one asked about her interests, her lifestyle, her personality, our relationship.

Only by then I would think, Thank god.

Because by then I had learned that whenever I talked about my sister, I was always telling two stories. One was an orderly, factual story that fell into some recognizable idea of what a person with special needs was like, and what it was like to be her sister. In other words, the surface story that didn't present too much of a challenge to people who, for whatever reason, didn't want to know more. The other story was all the rest—the details that upended the comfortable expectations, that presented a complex reality, and that revealed the difficult, messy, and even contradictory truths that writhed underneath. By my mid-thirties, I knew all too well that it was safer to suppress what I'll call the substory. I would think, How can I tell someone who imagines Beth to be a sweet, compliant, gullible angel who loves everyone, who will be taken advantage of by the big bad world, and indulges in pleasant hobbies like making potholders, that she's actually a bull-headed, loud-talking, tough-minded, socially courageous, stand-up-to-anyone, wily ball of energy? That she loves those who earn her love, except that sometimes, if they've stuck by her for awhile (like her sister), she acts like she doesn't? That she's given to speaking judgmentally, seeing herself as savvier, cooler, more deserving than many others (especially her sister)? That her life mission is spending all day, every day, riding city buses?

And that's only what they'd have found out if they'd asked about *her*. Heaven forbid they'd ask about *me*. Because then I'd have to say, Yes, I love her. But often I'm groping for some kind of enlightenment about how to act around my sister. Some kind of permanent answer. Because there are too many times when I feel angry or overwhelmed or hurt, and I don't know what to do.

That's not to say that I haven't found any answers to my many questions. Indeed, a bounty of answers came eight years ago, when she asked me to ride her buses for a year. Our relationship had been strained for two decades by then, so I agreed (substory: with reluctance). The year made an enormous difference. I came to see that part of our difficulty was derived from my judging her for her eccentric ways. First, her case manager, Olivia, introduced me to the civil rights concept of self-determination, which says that Beth has a right to make her own choices about her own life. Then Beth's bus driver friends demonstrated, through their acceptance of her quirky passion, both the rightness of self-determination and how to just let Beth be Beth. All along, Beth's boyfriend, Jesse, who shares her same disability, kept encouraging me, explaining in his gentle way, "Her mind is set. Like a clock. And no one can reset that clock."

After that year, I found myself on the far side of a huge mountain of emotional junk, one we'd spent a lifetime creating: my guilt at not being more actively involved in her life, her resentment of my impulse to boss her around, my embarrassment about her unconventional habits, her disinterest in anything about me, my anger at her self-centeredness, her sly manipulations so I'd open my wallet, my vexation about my underestimation of her cleverness, her disdain for my not being like her, and on and on. Finally, we simply enjoyed being together.

That's when we set up our current routine. That's when the friendships that I'd started during my year with her—with Jacob, Olivia, Jesse—blossomed. That's when I became her companion for medical events, like eye surgery. She called four times a day, on an 800 number I got to spare her a bill. She wrote four letters a day. I visited all the time, we celebrated holidays with the drivers, and sometimes she even asked how I was.

Since then, we've formed a new routine. Now, about once a month, we rendezvous inside the waiting room at this bus center. Unlike today, the waiting room is usually where Beth waits for me, in the air conditioning or heat, near the vending machines and bathroom, talking to security guards and passengers. When I arrive, she'll be looking out the plate glass windows toward the bus lanes, fingering a plastic bag that contains her new homemade card for me. I'll cross the room toward her, passing riders of all ages, knowing that, although they're not paying attention, almost all of them are familiar with my sister.

Beth is, perhaps needless to say, a well-known character in this city. If you sat down in any fast food restaurant and brought her up, everyone around you would nod. She's the woman with some mental disability who wears brightly colored clothes, is always on the buses, and was once nationally famous. Some townspeople admire her love of life; others roll their eyes at her incessant chatter. Occasionally, after she thrusts the bagged card at me in the bus center, she introduces me to the friendly ones, or the ones who want to be writers. But then she'll quickly move along with our routine, hustling me outside to a gate where I'll have thirty seconds to meet a new driver or hug one I already know, then hurrying me out to my car, where we'll drive to Wal-Mart and the grocery store. So I don't get to meet the ones who look down their nose at Beth.

But whenever we leave the waiting room, I'll often feel people glance at us. This is, though, not just because some of them look askance at Beth. It's also because Beth's national fame came because of me. After I rode the buses with Beth, I wrote a book about our experience. The book became an unlikely best seller, then a Hallmark Hall of Fame movie, and for the last few years I've traveled around the country, talking to hundreds of groups about Beth's right to live the life she wants. She became, for some people, the embodiment of self-determination, while I became the embodiment of the typical sister who'd worked through her difficulties with her sib.

It's true that the bus ride did fuse us back together. But to my dismay, a few years after our long ride, several variables shifted. These are the substories—the dark truths—I rarely even tell my closest friends. Suddenly, sadly, Jesse developed emotional problems. For reasons I could not ascertain or define, and that broke my heart, he went from being a reliable, thoughtful, tranquil individual to someone who could, in the blink of an eye, turn surly, even hostile. He became erratic about keeping commitments to join our visits, prompting Beth to spend our time together pleading that we drive around to find him—not because she feared for his safety, but because she wanted to force him to come along, regardless of the mood he was in, regardless of how miserable his unpredictability, and their confusing dynamics, made me. At the same time, Beth developed a series of infatuations with new drivers, becoming so caught up that at times when I drove to see her, she'd tell me to wait while she rode around until their shift came to an end.

This period also coincided with both of our parents developing the kind of illnesses that beset elderly people, and, even though I'd been the most involved family member for years, I was disheartened by how little interest she expressed in their well-being, even refusing to buy a phone card to call our mother until I shelled out the seven dollars. I would talk to Beth about my growing despondency with our visits, but nothing would improve. So paradoxically, as I grew closer to Jacob and Olivia, eventually counting them among my best friends, I struggled more and more to let things roll off my back when I was around my sister.

So new questions supplanted the old. Instead of wondering why others didn't ask about her, or how I could accept her myself, I wondered how to get through visits that left me frazzled and depressed. And I'd wonder what was wrong with me: how could I *still* be asking questions at all?

It's now 12:18, and here I am, nearing Bus Stop 4, where Beth is waiting. Her eyes lock onto mine as I come up to her. "Hi," I say. "I made it on time."

"Here," she says, and immediately hoists a plastic bag from beside her feet and motions for me to look inside. I almost do, but first I want at least some gesture of affection. When I spent that year riding with her, Beth admitted that she doesn't like to be touched, so for awhile I didn't try anymore. I didn't mind, because she was always so pleased to see me that sometimes she initiated one anyway.

But for these last few years, she's dispensed with greetings entirely, as she did just now. I can view this as eagerness to get to the matter at hand, which is, today, for me to look into the plastic bags. But I can also view it as disregard for me, for my concern for her, for the time I take to drive here, for the loyalty I have toward her, for the effort I put into getting along with her. Often I see it both ways at the same time, which is what I do right now. I also tell myself not to be bothered that she doesn't acknowledge me with a boisterous hello, or even a halfhearted, *Did you have a good trip?* After all, in the superficial version of this story, the one where I, as the sister, rotate around her needs, I should be able to laugh off the absence of a hello, a question about my well-being, a hug. I should be so content with my role in her life that my desires should have no bearing on my feelings. Sometimes I really can do this, but sometimes I want to be, well, a sister. Someone who, in addition to being a chauffeur, doctor's assistant, and bank machine, is also someone worth a greeting.

Now here's another substory. At times, when I feel this longing, I don't always do the saintly thing. Instead I ignore what *she* wants, which is what I do right now, and I put an arm around her shoulder and give a squeeze. It's not a full-fledged hug, but it's more than no hug at all. She remains stiff, arms at her sides, but at least I've shown the love that, despite it all, I feel, and that I wish she would show me, in a way that I want. The moment where our bodies touch is not satisfying in the slightest. Nor is it the story I will tell friends if they ask me (and few of them will) about my visits with Beth. But it is the truth: that, even after a year on the buses, a book, a movie, and the world's impression that I actually know what to do as a sister, our visit has begun as it has for the past two years, as a push-me/pull-you of wills.

Then boom—it's 12:20. Jacob arrives right on the dot, his face brightening when he spies me through the windshield. We wait for his passengers to file off, then Beth and I follow him to the drivers' room, where we present him with the plastic bags, which I did indeed look inside, and praise, just before his arrival. There are gifts she's wrapped for him (paid for by a collection she took up from other drivers), purple napkins and plates and forks, his favorite turkey sandwich for his lunch, and a cake with purple lettering that says, "Happy Birthday Jacob."

We laugh and enjoy ourselves, offering slices to other drivers, talking about the songs on the CDs that Jacob just opened. Then we go out for a drive in Jacob's car—he has only half an hour before his break ends, and he wants to show me his new bus route, which culminates at what he describes as an exquisite fountain, rising high and majestic above that part of the city, restoring him with hope at the end of every run. He pops in the CD, and we almost turn onto the road to the fountain. But Beth says that a store on the other side of town is having a sale on paper towels that one of her neighbors needs, so we go there first. Then we drive to Jesse's apartment so she can drop off a slice of cake. It becomes clear that the fountain will have to wait.

Even so, I am genuinely happy as we spend this time together, and in ways that are in complete agreement with the more surface story. Jacob is as fun and kind and truly interested in us as I would want any friend to be. Beth is as endearing and fanciful and truly giving as I would want any loved one to be. I can think of nothing more wonderful than to be here right now with my sister.

But there is a substory, even underneath this moment. I think of it as Jacob's car passes one of the city's nicer restaurants. It is a substory that Beth does not know and would never guess, but that gave me yet a few more of those answers which, over and over, I find myself seeking.

Two years ago, I took Olivia out to this restaurant for her birthday. I hadn't expected to unburden myself to her, but as we relaxed into the meal, I found myself sharing all the substories I hadn't been telling. The trouble I was having with Jesse. The anger and hurt I felt toward Beth. The frustration that, the more I gave, the more disdainful she became. How could I honor her choices about her own life without making my own needs disappear?

Olivia and I talked a long time. At first we considered trying to find a family counselor who would see Beth and me. But we knew that very few people in the therapeutic professions are attuned to the complexities of special sibling relationships. The few times I'd mentioned Beth in counseling, in my teens and twenties, the whole topic was just glossed over—and that was despite how much, even then, I was torn between a sense of responsibility and pride toward her, and despair over how our difficulties sometimes brought me pain.

Then Olivia remembered that she'd once worked with a therapist who had experience with, as the expression went, "people with challenging behaviors." As soon as she got back from lunch, she called and asked if he'd speak to me.

The very first session I then had with Dr. Michael, over the phone, gave me a new round of answers. He listened thoroughly as I spilled all the substories, and when I finished he assured me that even people who think they've figured it out often find that, for reasons they might never understand, they sometimes end up back at square one. He said that a lot of my concerns were common, and were often expressed by the professionals he dealt with. Then he said, "It can get better. But for that to happen, you have to change."

I already knew this, from my time on the bus with Beth. But that change had concerned my attitude about her choices. The change Dr. Michael urged was about my actions. The first change amounted to accepting my sister. The second change amounted to respecting myself.

First, he asked why I wanted to be a part of Beth's life. I told him that I just felt I had to be, and anyway, she often asked me to visit. So this was not a negotiable issue.

Then he asked why I wanted to be a part of Jesse's life. I told him that I was fond of Jesse, and that Beth wanted him along on our visits. But his behavior had gotten inexplicable to me. I'd suggested he see a doctor but he'd refused, and I often went home feeling horrible.

Then Dr. Michael said that respecting Beth's desires didn't mean that our time together had to be entirely about me fulfilling her choices no matter what. I could also acknowledge that I had my own limits. So, for instance, if I came to visit Beth and we'd already agreed to go to Wal-Mart with Jesse but he didn't show up, and suddenly she wanted to spend the visit driving around looking for him, I could say, "That isn't what we agreed on." If she still insisted, I could say, "We can continue to Wal-Mart, or I can go home. You can decide. And we can sit in the car for the whole visit until you decide. Those are the choices." If she *still* wanted to find him, I could say, "That's not one of the choices."

But what about seeing Jesse?

Dr. Michael said, "You feel a sense of responsibility toward your sister. Jesse isn't your sister. You can take a break from him until he works through whatever's going on with him."

I was relieved at these words, though saddened. Dr. Michael said, "Look, it will get worse before it gets better. But just stay calm. When you limit the choices, or tell Beth you need a break from Jesse, don't shout. Don't let yourself get sucked into drama. You're sisters— you know how to press each other's buttons. As soon as that starts, stop. Go to the bathroom. Get off the phone. Break the pattern. And it will get better. I promise."

I finished our call with hope. Knowing that someone understood the level of difficulty I was having was heartening. But having concrete ideas almost brought me to tears—just like when Olivia and Jacob had given me answers, too.

Immediately, I tried Dr. Michael's ideas, and others that he taught me in later calls. Although I felt a great loss when I backed away from Jesse, and although things did get worse before they got better, they got better. Not perfect. Not even close to perfect. But better enough to make me enjoy the next two years of visits with my sister. Two years that continue today.

I look at my watch. 2:45. We're in the grocery store now, having left Jacob at the bus center, and made the rounds at Wal-Mart. We're in line, about to pay for the cases of soda that are too heavy for Beth to take on the bus. The cashier says hello to Beth (the world seems more respectful toward my sister these days, and when it isn't, she asserts herself until it gets with the program), and begins to ring us up. I imagine the cashier glancing my way, then realizing, by the way we look and act, that we're sisters—sisters where one of us has a disability. But she can't see anything except that surface piece of information, and probably can't know what it means.

Then I look at the cashier a little harder. She's wearing a yellow plastic bracelet, the kind that honors a loved one with cancer. So the cashier has her own substory, I think, as Beth double-bags her sodas, and I remember the answer I came to years ago about why people didn't ask about Beth. I was an adult then, and had come to understand that everyone has some secret reality that's messy and contradictory and about as far from the surface as possible. And I realized then that at least some people didn't ask about Beth because they were too overwhelmed about their own lives to ask—or so unable to deal with their own substory that they didn't have room for ours.

I'll never know for sure, and the truth is probably different for each person. But just remembering that answer—one in a long chain of answers that I've reached in my life—I understand something more, as Beth runs ahead of me out of the store, checking the coin return on every pay phone for loose change: this journey with my sister will never be simple. There will always be a substory. And, like everyone with a substory, I will always have questions. Sometimes I'll get answers, and they'll really make a difference. But then something will happen and I'll be asking new questions. Again and again and again.

I think about this as I drive Beth back toward the bus center: The journey seems so endless, and sometimes, when I'm struggling for new answers, impossibly hard. Yet as every visit begins with a negotiation of wills, every visit ends with a commitment to keep moving ahead.

Then something happens that surprises me. Beth probably didn't plan it either. But here it is, as I pull up to the curb outside the bus center, and Beth finishes a story about a smelly passenger she can't stand. She slows her pace for the first time since I arrived and says, "Why do you bother with me?"

I'm stunned; she's never asked me anything like this. What should I say? Despite my own slow pace, a million answers rage through my mind. Because it's the right thing to do. Because I couldn't live with myself if I didn't. Because I love you. Yet to my further surprise, what comes out of my mouth is a question. I ask Beth, "What do you think?"

"The drivers say it's because you care."

A wetness hits my eyes like a storm. I say, "What do *you* think?"

"I think they're right." And then she adds the words I never thought I'd hear from her. She says, "They say you're a good sister. I think that's right, too."

"Oh, Beth," I say, and I can barely see, my eyes are suddenly so full.

A moment later, Beth hurries into the bus center. Still at the curb, I call my husband to let him know I'm on my way, and then, as I pull onto the street and a bus passes by—the bus where she's now sitting with another driver—I think about how much I want the big, final, fountain of an answer, the one that will restore my hope forever, that will make every visit go smoothly until the end of eternity. But life with my sister is not a transcendent joy. It's a long, long bus route, with stops at one question, then another and another, until it finally reaches its destination of answers. But then it just heads out again the next morning, stopping at a whole new series of questions. Some days the ride proves sunnier than others. Some days I meet a Jacob or an Olivia or a Dr. Michael along the way. Some days my sister even hugs me when I say hello.

Her bus pulls ahead of my car, and I follow behind. At the next intersection, she goes right, and I go left. Through the city I continue, into the fading afternoon, telling myself not to forget this day, this moment, when I finally grasp the impermanence of enlightenment. When I finally know that I will never reach the fountain.

Dusk is falling when I turn onto the entrance ramp for the highway. I glance at her card on the seat beside me, the *I love you, sis* bright in day-glow markers. Happy and sad, hopeful and longing, I press the accelerator and get up to speed and aim my car toward home.

* * *

Rachel Simon *is best known for her memoir* Riding the Bus with My Sister, *which was adapted for a Hallmark Hall of Fame movie. She is also the author of several books of fiction and nonfiction, and will be publishing a follow-up memoir in May 2009. Currently writing full-time, Rachel lives in Delaware with her husband, Hal. To learn more about Rachel, her books, and her tips on writing, please go to www.rachelsimon.com.*

24.
A Mom on Many Levels

Libby Gondry

It seemed like we had waited forever for Dad to come home with news, when, at long last, he arrived. All seven kids sat on the stairs in the front hall, eager to hear what Dad had to report. It was odd: he didn't look happy or sad. We had a new sister, Dad told us, but there was a problem: she was born with Down syndrome and doctors didn't think she would live past four years. The doctors recommended that we place her in an institution. We all agreed with our parents: bringing her home was the only thing to do.

Life did change at home. Our sister's health and schooling got a lot of attention. That was natural. But, it got difficult for me when I was always told to bring my sister with me on play dates, trips to the park, or visits with my friends. When I was ten, I brought my sister to a friend's house and while playing on their swing set, Phoebe fell and broke her leg. It wasn't a simple break and she ended up in a body cast from chest to ankle. And, I was told it was my fault. I should have somehow known better and not let her on that chair swing.

My perception and position in life changed entirely from that moment on. I was not a kid anymore. I was a caretaker. To try to recapture the love of my parents, which I felt was gone, I did everything in my power to take care of Phoebe and be the best sister I could. And I became a helper, a person who did things, but never again the person who openly sought or got attention, love, or validation.

My father and my sister Patty, who was my best friend, died when I was thirteen. It was sudden and shocking. More shocking to me was how my life changed yet again. Gone was the one person who protected me from my mother's mood swings, and gone was the one person I could talk to about anything. And, again, my mother blamed me. This time I, also, blamed myself. I should have been on the boat that they died on, but Mom hadn't allowed me to go because she was mad at me for something. I haven't a clue now what I did to get the punishment, but the result was I was alive and my sister wasn't.

My mother experienced events right out of the Book of Job. Before Phoebe was born, my seven-year-old brother was killed by a neighbor child playing with his father's gun. And to lose a husband and eleven-year-old daughter to a boating accident caused my mother to experience major depression. Mom ran Dad's business for a little while, and then sold out.

By the time I was fifteen, all of my siblings were out of the house except for Phoebe, so I was the one who listened to my mother crying many nights. I was the one who did the grocery shopping (on my bike), cleaning, gardening, etc. Anyone with a house knows what it takes to run it; I was doing that for Mom. And anyone who has siblings with a disability knows what it takes to keep them going, and I did what needed to be done for Mom from the moment I got my driving permit. I drove my sister to her horseback riding twice a week, bowling, dances, and speech lessons three times a week across town.

Mom spent weeks at a time in her room. I brought her coffee and meals, clean laundry, the mail, and anything else she wanted. I did this in secret so Mom would not be embarrassed. I had lost a father, my best friend, and sister. All my older siblings moved on to their new lives. And, by the time I was fifteen years old, for all intents and purposes, I had lost a mother and became a surrogate mother to my sister. Telling anyone would be betraying my mom and family, so I lived with this alone.

I became invisible as an individual in the family. My other siblings were brought up and taught that they were intelligent, interesting, important people. Their college expenses were paid for and they were given black-tie parties, a junior year abroad, and big weddings. My mother was so tired and depressed by the time I got to high school, she couldn't handle even being a mother to me.

Mom had lost loved ones to death, and lost children who grew up and moved out. She couldn't control my sister's temper or her growth or lack of development, so the only thing she had left was to control me. It seemed nothing was good enough, although I kept trying.

I was told my grades were horrible, but when I went through Mom's papers after she died, I compared my high school grades to my siblings' and discovered that they were almost identical. I loved to sing, but my mother ignored my musical talents. I had twice been accepted to sing at the Kennedy Center for the Performing Arts in high school. They were huge events in my life, but not important to my mother. She didn't come to see me the first time, and only came to see me the second time because a family friend wanted to see the concert. Appearances were so important. We were always told by Mom to have a happy face in public no matter what was going on at home.

I took any attention I could get from her. I still have diaries full of lists of things I did every day for Mom; I just prayed that one day I would be someone special to her. Being the only sibling left home with Phoebe and Mom was no fun. The joy in life had simply left by age thirteen. And thus began my ongoing struggle with weight. I was so scared through high school and felt so put down, my joy and solace only came through eating secretly in my room.

The unfairness of things at home really started to get to me when I went away to college. I rebelled, but, of course, my rebellion only hurt me. I skipped classes and eventually quit school. At twenty-one, I was tired, the most tired student I knew, both emotionally and psychologically. While I was still in school, I usually worked two jobs and went home for every break to help Mom. At school, I was afraid to answer the phone for fear it would be my mother calling to complain about how she needed help, how selfish I was for leaving her, or why I didn't call more often. The only good thing I did for myself that year was to tell my mother that I would no longer tolerate being hit by her.

I met my husband in college, and because he gave me the love that I hadn't felt in years, I was happy to quit school and marry him. He not only gave me a way out of sadness and inadequacy, but for the first time in a very long time, helped me feel like I was *a Person*. Yes, Person with a capital letter. In the movie *Cinderfella*, Jerry Lewis talks of Persons and People. Persons were those who were special and important. People were, well, just all others. And, my husband made me feel like a special Person.

Only two years later, I was again called to be my mother's daughter and Phoebe's sister when Mom was struck with cancer. For the next two years, I traveled over several states to care for Mom and Phoebe during Mom's chemo treatments. After two years of leaving my family for weeks at a time, Mom's health deteriorated rapidly. One day I got a call from Phoebe's school telling me that Mom was in the hospital, and they didn't know what to do with my sister. I had to arrange for Phoebe to spend that night with a sister who lived nearer by, and then I jumped on a plane to Washington, D.C. with my five-year-old daughter. The doctors told us Mom couldn't be alone anymore. My husband and I dropped everything to return to Florida to find and move into a house that would accommodate our growing family, as well as Phoebe and my gravely ill mother. During the short time Mom lived following the move, she begged me to care for my sister, and never put her in an institution or home.

And yet again, life changed dramatically. I now had full responsibility for a twenty-four year-old woman with the mental development of a two-year-old. I needed to find her employment and activities and care for her health. We had to adjust to living with a large person who had toddler-style temper tantrums. We had to teach our children what Phoebe could and couldn't understand. And we had to make sure that our kids weren't overshadowed by Phoebe as I had been. How does one keep a promise like the one Mom asked of me, especially when life has other plans? Phoebe lived with us for a year and half until my husband's employer, the U.S. Navy, transferred us to Spain. We agreed to the move because our brother volunteered to care for her. But, his (now ex-) wife had a change of heart, and no other sibling stepped up to the plate, so Phoebe ended up in a group home. In three years, I returned from Spain and I sought to have Phoebe live with us again. Extracting her from her vile group home was a seven-year battle—and the hardest thing I have ever done. Her caregivers didn't keep her clean, didn't stop her from overeating, didn't take her to activities, and didn't attend to her health. Phoebe spent almost all of her time in her room, sometimes not even being called to eat. This terrible home had the backing of the judge, probate commissioner, DDD representative, the Goodwill store where Phoebe worked, and—a shock to me—one of our sisters.

I would fly from our home in Illinois to Oregon for hearings in the probate court. Why probate? Because the horrible will our mother had when she died in 1988 left her estate in probate as long as Phoebe lives and it can't be settled until her passing. It left the courts to oversee the dispensation of the funds left for Phoebe's care. And, frankly, the will gave too much power to people who have no interest in Phoebe's well-being and is subject to the selfishness and greed of people with little conscience.

We finally won in court and Phoebe moved in with us again, and has been with us for seven years now. I have never blamed Phoebe for anything that happened in my life. She caused none of it. Who's to say that my mother would have been any different if Phoebe hadn't been part of the mix? Phoebe can be funny, friendly, sweet, helpful, and loving. She can also be a pain, angry, frustrating, maddening, and a trial. But, can't all siblings be that way? Our relationship is more of a mom/daughter one because of her developmental level, but we have our sister moments. If I kiss my husband in front of her, she will say "eeuww," her way of saying, "get a room." Or, sometimes she will hand me a napkin as if she's telling me to wipe my mouth! But, for the most part it's me taking care of her like a child, reminding her about simple things over and over: use soap in the shower, change your clothes when they're dirty, blow your nose, etc.

My history had made me into the person I am. Over the years, I have had no confidence in myself because my mother had emotionally and physically abused me. I had no sense of who I was or who I could be. I had been told for so many years that the only good I could ever be in this life is someone who takes care of others, starting with Mom and Phoebe. That is one reason why I have been an active volunteer for the last twenty-three years, often in a leadership role. I am good at it. I have gotten so many awards I have lost count, but the accolades have never compensated for the love lost by deaths in my teens and twenties, or by remaining family members who did not care or attempt to understand.

On the flip side, I did come away with a firm idea of how I would like my own family to be, what kind of mother I wanted to be, and what kind of relationships I would foster in my own children as siblings. After just celebrating my twenty-fifth wedding anniversary, I look at my children: they show love toward each other, their parents, and the world; they have confidence in themselves to try to reach for their dreams; they know that no matter what, their parents are 100 percent behind them. I feel I have succeeded with them.

What the future holds is one of my biggest worries. What happens if Phoebe's health deteriorates? Right now she's mobile, but what if that changes? What if she gets Alzheimer disease, as many adults with Down syndrome do? I just don't know if I have the strength to go through that with her. She is younger than I and in good health. What happens if I die before her? I really don't want my children tied down to her care as I have been. I want them to be free to do anything and go anywhere. My other siblings don't have anything to do with Phoebe, so that's not an option that I see. For now, my husband and I will continue to support and care for Phoebe, and try hard not to worry about all the tomorrows and their uncertainty.

* * *

After growing up in Washington, D.C., attending college in Indiana, and spending twenty years moving around the world as a U.S. Navy wife, **Libby Gondry** *currently resides in Auburn, Washington. She* *has four children and has been married for twenty-five years. Libby has followed her passion of helping people have a better life by being a "professional volunteer" and has tried to make every place she has lived a little better than it was when she found it. Most volunteering has been as an innovator of creative community projects, chairperson, or board member. She has also been a Navy Ombudsman for seven years. Libby is the seventh of nine siblings. Her sister Phoebe, who has Down syndrome, lives with Libby and her family. Libby loves to listen to high school bands and choirs, is an avid canasta player, and loves to travel, but her primary passion is her family.*

25.
Kep

Kim Keprios

Kep, Kepper, Miguel, Eggo—all names with a story behind it, wrapped in love and affection for my brother Mike. He's fifty-two—I am fifty. He has more gray hair than I do and I have a lot more wrinkles than he does!

Michael George Keprios, the second of five kids. As a mom myself, I can't imagine the emotions and pressures that must have engulfed my parents when Mike was born in 1955, with no eyes, and according to their trusted physician, severe mental retardation. With Mike deemed likely never able to walk or talk, my folks were advised to institutionalize him. And yet with all the courage, compassion, and commitment they could muster, Dodie and George Keprios brought their son Mike home to be raised alongside his siblings.

I know life was not easy for my parents. Little support existed in the fifties and sixties for people with intellectual and developmental disabilities and their families. But life did seem normal because it was all we knew.

Mike needed care 24/7. I would play airplane with him at breakfast, load up his spoon with Raisin Bran, and zoom it into his mouth for an on-target landing. We had good laughs over this routine and inevitably there was more cereal *on* Mike than *in* him. He eventually learned to dress, toilet, and feed himself, but one of us always needed to be within helping distance.

Affectionate, funny, the epitome of unconditional love, patient, tolerant, a musical trivia genius and Country and Western music fanatic, a lover of the Minnesota Twins, pizza, hot dogs, pickles, and family celebrations. Mike has bionic hearing and a comedian's timing with his injections of humor. And like the infamous W.C. Fields, he could do without screaming kids and dogs.

Though Mike's tests suggest he is quite challenged intellectually, he has a memory that could win him millions on *Jeopardy*. Our family has always celebrated many traditions. One of these is my dad and Mike reading *'Twas the Night Before Christmas* on Christmas Eve as we wait for the arrival of Santa Claus. Mind you, Mike only hears this story once a year, but for as long as I can remember, he has been able to recite the entire story verbatim, with my dad giving a word here or there as a cue. He also knows every obscure hymn we sing at church and, with the hint of one or two notes, can launch into the full lyrics of any Country and Western song he hears on the radio.

My favorite tradition with Mike is our annual visit to the state fair, fondly known as the "Great Minnesota Get-Together." Each year Kep, my husband, John, and I go to the Grandstand concert for some country twang. Mike has successfully converted me to an occasional fan by introducing me to the Dixie Chicks, Martina McBride, Alabama—the list is longer than I would like to admit. We stomp and holler and sing too loud and off-key—and we fit right in!

Mike's story is like that of so many others I have met through the Arc. No services, barriers to services, frustration, segregation, social isolation, and loneliness. And a million and one good things are also part of the story—good people who believe in him, support him, love him. And opportunities in Mike's life that I am sure my parents could never have imagined back in 1955.

My brother lives in a home with three roommates, within the "fifteen-minute rule" of his family (somehow my mother has managed to keep her crew close by, and as we age, we are all coming to appreciate this unwritten Keprios law). He works at Old Chicago Pizza, a job he is proud of and where he is rewarded constantly by the waft of pizza fumes swirling around him—one of his favorite food groups. He swims twice a week, does the treadmill if bribed creatively, is a regular at Baker's Square Restaurant, goes to church with me when he feels like it, enjoys concerts, listens to the Minnesota Twins games on the radio and cheers whether they are winning or losing, watches *Leave It To Beaver* and *Andy Griffith* reruns, volunteers at Arc's Value Village Thrift Store, and celebrates every Hallmark holiday ever invented with his family.

Indeed, Mike's life has been a rollercoaster of ups and downs, but through it all he perseveres, forgives, and maintains a joyful heart. Life is good.

Mike has been the anchor in our family—on rare occasions feeling like a weight that ties me down when I yearn for the freedom to "leave home." But mostly an anchor in the best sense of the word. Mike has always brought our family together—kept us laughing, grounded in a perspective and reality that is based in gratitude, faith, trust, and love.

Mike led me to a career path I may otherwise never have pursued, or been afforded the opportunities I have had through my twenty-five years with Arc Greater Twin Cities. At the core he is behind the passion and sense of urgency I bring to my work in advocacy for people with disabilities and their families.

I feel indebted to Mike for bringing meaning and purpose to my life, and do not for a minute take for granted that my work with the "Arc Family" has been a huge blessing, filled with ample rewards and challenges. My spouse and closest friends, and people I would likely have never have had the chance to know—all came into my life because of Arc, because of Mike.

Now my dear brother and I are on the official AARP membership rolls at fifty and fifty-two. And for the first time, my worries for him have moved to the forefront in a way that only comes with the awareness that our parents were right—we are not immortal. My biggest fear is that Mike will outlive his siblings. He is the healthiest of the Keprios crew and does not appear to show the wear and tear of fifty years the same way the rest of us are doing.

I, of course, have a very long list of other worries that keep me up at night. How will Mike handle the death of our parents, when they are still his number one request for whom to visit on the weekend? Will he ever have a real friend outside his paid staff? Does he get enough attention, conversation, affection? How will he age—will he lose his mobility? Will I be able to get him up our stairs and into the shower? Will I have the strength and mobility to be there for him as he needs me to be?

Will his staff remember to cut up his grapes and hot dogs so he does not choke? Will they stand by to make sure he does not burn himself with the hot water faucet? Will they check on him during a thunderstorm—a frightening ruckus for him to endure? Does he sit alone in his room too much? Does the phone ever ring for him outside of family calling? How can I ever be sure he is truly safe?

From the little day-to-day idiosyncrasies to the monumental life issues that must be faced with Mike, I worry.

I also worry about what I would do if Mike were to die before me. I can't imagine the void that would emerge with him gone. He fills me up with worry, but much more with joy—with the true unconditional love we yearn for—with the daily reminder about trusting and putting faith in others—the real meaning of interdependence. Because even though Mike may need 24/7 support in some ways, he gives to others so many intangible gifts in a twenty-four hour period, it is truly a reciprocal relationship for me with him, and I suspect all the lucky ones in his path.

Life with a sibling like Kep is without a doubt a gift that brings headaches and heartaches. It is humbling and often hilarious, sometimes all at the same time.

* * *

Kim Keprios joined Arc Hennepin County in 1982 as Community Services Director and was promoted to Executive Director in 1986. She continued in this role through the merger of Arc Hennepin and Carver counties in 2001, and in 2006 was named the Chief Executive Officer of Arc Greater Twin Cities. She has advanced many initiatives to improve the lives of people with intellectual and developmental disabilities and their families, and has been honored for leadership excellence by the national and state Arc chapters. In addition to her work with Arc, Kim has been active with the Greater Twin Cities United Way throughout her career, including service on United Way's Board of Directors and chair of the Council of Agency Executives. A Twin Cities native with degrees from the University of Minnesota and St. Thomas University, Kim enjoys cross-country skiing, snowshoeing, biking, and hiking with her husband and son.

26.
Surprises

Nora Fox Handler with Margaret Fox-Hawthorne

We were taken aback at Mom's wake when our thirty-three-year-old brother, Michael, said, "Why didn't my mother ever tell me I was retarded?" That was the first of many surprises over the last ten years since our mom passed away. Some of these surprises were amusing and good, but most were depressing or at least stress producing.

We have three brothers with developmental disabilities and all three lived with our mom until she passed away in 1998. Our brother Marty, who did not have a diagnosis or any services, worked on the family farm, a horse-boarding stable. Patrick and Michael went to a sheltered workshop each day, and that was the extent of the services they received.

We knew it would be a mess when Mom died. She did not—and would not—include us in her plans for our brothers' futures. She told us everything was all set, and, after her death, the next big surprise was how wrong she was. We wonder if we should have tried harder. Could we have talked her into including us or at least showing us the (ultimately worthless) special needs trust she had made?

Working in a crisis mode—and with little knowledge of how to get help and services—we tried to find new ways to support and house our brothers. What do you do with three brothers who live on a farm that must be sold to pay inheritance taxes? How do you care for three brothers when you have families of your own, careers, and aging parents and in-laws who also need support?

We started by taking turns staying overnight with Marty, Patrick, and Michael while trying to sell the farm and parcel responsibilities previously managed by Mom. Margaret, who worked full time and had her own family to raise, oversaw the estate and the horse-boarding business. As she lived an hour from the farm, she spent much time in the car. I lived three hours away and cared for our brothers almost every weekend for six months. Our three other sisters helped as they could and took some of the weeknight shifts.

Our next step was to move the brothers off the farm. Marty lived with my family while we sought a proper diagnosis and services. Patrick lived with our sister Kathleen, a widow with two young daughters and a chronic disease. Michael moved in with Margaret and her family during construction of an addition to their home intended to make room for the brothers.

During that time I was surprised by how much I did not know about my brothers. I was not familiar with their likes and dislikes, some of their quirky habits, and how much they were able to do on their own.

Ten years later, the guys are all living away from family—yet another surprise. I don't think we ever really pictured them living away from family. Marty, who was eventually diagnosed with high functioning autism, has his own apartment and is the most independent. Patrick and Michael live in different group homes, in different nearby towns.

After having the three brothers live with Margaret, Kathleen, and me—and later, all three with Margaret and her family—we thought it would be easier once they were all living away from family. But that has not been the case. Being the guardian of Pat and Mike, representative payee and financial counselor for Marty, and the trustee of the family trust is at least a part-time job for Margaret.

She is lucky if the guys have the same caseworker for six months and there are constant phone calls, forms to fill out, and much driving between their three locations. These responsibilities, in addition to a full time job, leave Margaret with very little time for herself.

Probably the biggest surprise was the severity of our brother Michael's mental illness and the impact that would have on him and his family. According to his doctors, Michael has a schizo-affective disorder and an intellectual disability. We did not realize that our brother was having visual and auditory hallucinations until he moved in with Margaret and her family. His mental illness worsened to the extent that he was hospitalized three times in six months. He had periods when he was keeping Margaret up at night because he was psychotic and could not sleep. We began to fear for his safety and Margaret's health. When an opening came up in a dual diagnosis group home run by his agency, we grabbed the placement, fearing that at some point he might end up anywhere in the state as an emergency placement. He's not as happy in his group home as he was living with Margaret, but he has adjusted pretty well and most of the staff seems to be caring and competent. The fact that he and his other brothers live nearby makes it easier to check on them, have them visit, or take them on outings.

There have been positives during these last ten years. We've certainly gotten to know our brothers much better and appreciate their different personalities. We have met many wonderful people who have helped and supported us in our journey with our brothers. We are now much better at supporting them and not sweating the small stuff.

Where Marty is with his life is yet another surprise, and on most days, this is a good thing. I really don't think any of his family would have pictured him living in his own place and advocating for himself and his girlfriend. Yes, my brother has found love and is in a long-term relationship. When he started dating he was living in my basement and I was freaking out. His first girlfriend came over to visit and I did everything possible to keep them from being alone. I knew that Marty had never had sex and I was afraid that if he did, it would be like opening Pandora's box. The other thing I was afraid of was Marty fathering a child. It became my mission that Marty would not lose his virginity on my watch. My husband thought I was crazy and should just stay out of it, but I managed to keep the relationship from advancing to physical intimacy with the help of his girlfriend's sister, who shared my view of the situation.

Then, when he went to live with Margaret, Marty met Gwen. The chemistry was immediate. Employed at the same workshop, both Marty and Gwen had trouble keeping things "appropriate." Marty's inappropriateness had to do with what he said, while Gwen was given to public displays of affection and occasional flashing. Not surprisingly, this led to a few issues with the staff. Marty was moved to a community job, which resolved the problem. Much to our family's relief, Marty agreed that he was not ready to be a father and chose to take care of that issue surgically.

The whole family knows the details of the day when Marty lost his virginity. He gave many people too much information on the big day; in fact, almost everyone who would listen learned the details. Then Marty wondered how Margaret and I found out since he had not told us. Now that Marty and Gwen have been together for over four years, they have both calmed down a bit and things seem good for them. Marty is Gwen's mentor and advocate and has contributed significantly to the quality of her life. Gwen has a state-appointed guardian, lives in a 100-bed facility that she hates, and has no family members who advocate for her. Marty has negotiated her spending weekends with him and helps her get out of her group home for outings on a regular basis. They have even considered marriage; his sisters, however, have a few reservations.

Regardless, Marty is doing his best to help Gwen get into a better living situation, and we are amazed and proud of all he has done for her. Marty has made a rich, full life for himself and Gwen—and he's done it on his own with nothing more than a little advice and financial assistance from his sisters. And if you asked him, he would probably tell you he did not need that advice.

Emerson wrote, "Life is a series of surprises, and would not be worth taking or keeping if it were not." Everyone in our family has been deeply affected by the often difficult and sometimes rewarding surprises brought about by our brothers' disabilities and our mother's unwillingness to discuss their future. We sisters have been surprised at how resilient families can be when there is no other option. Our brothers, we think, have been surprised at how independent they can be—if called upon to be so. And while we will always regret our mother's inability to plan for our brothers' future, we think she would be surprised at how far we all have come.

* * *

Nora Fox Handler is the treasurer and one of the founding members of SIBS Supporting Illinois Brothers and Sisters, a nonprofit support and advocacy organization for Illinois siblings. She serves on a number of boards and panels advocating and fundraising for people with disabilities and mental illness. Nora helps support her sister Margaret in her role as primary caregiver to their three adult brothers with developmental disabilities and mental illness. Along with her sister Margaret, Nora helped organize the first and second annual Adult Sibling Conference in McHenry, IL. She currently works as a service provider for Weight Watchers. In her spare time she is learning to blog and has posted a few disability-related diaries on the website Daily Kos.

Margaret Fox-Hawthorne is presently teaching at the junior high in the town where she resides. She is guardian of two of her three brothers and Representative Payee for all three men. After her mother passed away in 1998, her brothers lived with her and her family. Recently the last of her brothers moved to a nearby group home. Margaret is active in several environmental groups in Northern Illinois serving as a board member and chairman of several committees. She is actively involved with the Congregational Unitarian Church in her area. She serves on the Developmental Advisory committee of the agency her brothers are involved with and is co-chair of their major fundraiser. Margaret is an avid gardener and also raises free range poultry for meat and eggs.

27.
Sister Struggles

Kate Strohm

The inner struggle continues. When I am with my sister who has cerebral palsy, I joke and laugh and tend to her needs. I am the perfect sister. But inside I cannot shake the desire to scream, "No I don't want this! It shouldn't be this way!" For a lifetime, whenever I think of my sister, who has both intellectual and physical disabilities, my overwhelming feeling is one of loss—for her, for me, and for my parents.

My fifty-nine-year-old sister, Helen, has been in supported accommodation for some time now, as her needs became too difficult for my parents to manage. I feel relieved that her future is secure in a well-run facility. I have guardianship and will always be in her life, but I don't have the daily issues that many siblings have. I am lucky that my husband and two daughters accept her completely. She is an integral part of our family. For her, our little family is a constant source of pride and joy.

But I still struggle with our relationship. I wish we were closer. I hear other siblings talk of their wonderful relationships with brothers and sisters with special needs and what I experience is a mix of grief and guilt. When I collect my sister from the group home to take her to visit our family, she seems excited to see me, but beyond that, communication is difficult. She has no speech; instead, she uses limited signals and sounds to show what she wants. I often leave our get-togethers feeling frustrated and guilty—could I have done more to nurture the relationship? Will I ever find peace in my relationship with her? Why does she have to suffer so? This is a loss that goes deep and has been there forever.

Certainly there are moments of humor and surprise at her ability to know things. Her life is spent anticipating the future—Christmas, my birthday, hers, and everyone else's in the family. She can go on for weeks and weeks—how long it is until Christmas—it's in three months, in two months, next week. And how does she know it's my birthday next week? It is impossible to know exactly her intellectual capability. I don't allow myself to imagine what else goes on inside her head. What if she is aware of all her losses and all my blessings—my husband and daughters, my own home and career?

As a child, I was a "bad sister." I must have been "bad" because I often felt angry with my sister and sometimes wished she would disappear. It wasn't fair— she seemed to "get away" with many of the things I didn't. There seemed to be two sets of rules, one for her and one for me. She always seemed so much more important than me. On the other hand, she had so little and I had so much in comparison—how could I possibly feel angry with someone for whom I felt so much sympathy?

I also had to be the "good child," to not make things difficult for my parents. I could sense their pain and did not want to add to it. I felt embarrassed by my sister's appearance and behavior, but, as with other feelings, these too were tucked away. As a family, we were not able to do many of the things that other families did. Times when I went out with both my parents were rare but very special for me.

My parents had friends and close family who accepted and valued Helen. I largely kept my friends separate. During my teen years, in particular, and then into early adulthood, my friends had little to do with my sister; in fact I prevented them having too much contact for fear I would be judged alongside her. Today that fear is gone. There is a greater sense of pride and caring, along with an extreme protectiveness, but I still long for a different sister.

And now my mother has dementia so the family conversation is difficult all around. And I notice the losses even more. My mother gave so much care to my sister but now she doesn't know how. I watch the confusion on my sister's face as my mother tries to tend to her needs but doesn't quite "get it." I have been saying goodbye to my mother for some time now. Although it feels unfair that, after a lifetime of caring, she now struggles to have her mind remember, it also seems, in part, a natural progression in this "circle of life" we all journey through.

Not so with my sister, Helen. Her struggle has been there forever, and continues. When we take her to visit my mother's aged care facility, say, I need to repeat over and over to people passing by the same messages that she tries to convey with animated noises and gestures. "Her carer [caregiver] has been unwell" or "she is moving to a new workshop next week." Again and again, for fifty-plus years, I have been doing this. There is no natural order here. Instead, the roles of older and younger sibling have been blurred forever. The younger is the older—the carer and the protector.

As I lose my parents to old age, I am more and more conscious of wishing I had another sibling. I have no one with whom I can share my memories of childhood, no one to share nieces and nephews, no one to share my own aging and the responsibility of family. It feels very self-indulgent saying these things but the grief goes on and on. I spend a lot of time talking myself out of such feelings but it doesn't work very well. I wonder if I will ever reach a state of acceptance. I have no faith in an after-life but, in some ways, the dedication I used in my book, *Siblings,* written in 2002, still offers some comfort. "For Helen—next time, together, you and I will sing and dance with the fairies."

* * *

Kate Strohm is the founder and Director of Siblings Australia. The U.S. version of her book, Being the Other One, was published by Shambhala Press in 2005. Kate originally trained as a hospital scientist but later moved into health promotion and print and radio journalism. In 1999 she established Siblings Australia (www.siblingsaustralia. org.au) and, since then, the organization has been increasingly recognized for its work with families and professionals. The focus is on strengthening families through increasing awareness, understanding, and capabilities at three levels: with siblings directly; with parents; and with providers who, in turn, offer support to families. Information and support services take the form of written materials, workshops for families and providers, and a website. The organization also plays an important role in areas of research and advocacy to inform social policy makers about the needs of siblings. Kate lives in Adelaide, South Australia, with her husband and two daughters.

28.
Who Sings the Shower Song?

Tom Keating

"James, you need to take a shower today."

"I can't wanna take a shower."

"You have to take a shower."

"Why?"

"Because grown men start to smell bad if they don't."

"I'll ring people's door bells."

"Knock it off and take the shower."

"Who sings 'The Shower Song'?"

"I don't know who sings the freakin' shower song. Just get in the damn shower."

"Aah fucka."

And so it would go. It wasn't like James dislikes showering, really. He loves water and swimming, and really digs music. He actually seems to enjoy showers once he starts, and seems to like being clean afterward. I had to learn that it was really a dance about power and control. But it took me a long time to get that, and he knows the dance better than I do. I always feel like he's a step ahead. "No flies on him," Mom likes to say.

James has told me any number of times, "You don't want to control me" and, "You can't want to tell me what to do" in his own unique linguistic style. Maybe, using his Jamesian logic and knowledge of music, he figured that if it was important, someone would have done a song about it. And Bobby Darin may have sung about taking a bath, but he didn't mention anything about showers, so James didn't need to bother taking one. Hard to know. At the beginning I'm not sure I gave him full credit for having logic, intelligence, and emotions and being a full psychological being. The things he did were all just "behaviors" that I needed to deal with.

There was a lot I had yet to learn—who he is, how he thinks, what he needs—when we flew from the Bronx back to Oregon in the summer of '81 at the beginning of this brotherly adventure of living together. We sat three across in our too-small airline seats—our brother Francis on the window, me on the aisle, and James wedged between us, eating our entrees. And then at 35,000 feet, for some reason, it seemed important to me that James eat his peas. Airline peas for chrissake. But dang it, this is where we start doing things differently. "James, why don't you eat your peas?"

Wham, wham, wham, wham. A boxer-quick series of smacks to the seatback in front of him. Man, for a 225-pound guy with autism standing about 5'4", he's fast! Umm, yah, sorry about that, sir. Yup, everything's okay here. (James, what the hell was *that* about?) Okaaay, so I guess we just won't worry about the peas for now, but you wait. The times they are a changin' my man.

The rest of the flight wasn't really much better, and I was pretty fried when we landed in SF. Crisp is probably more like it. Rental car hassles were just another log on the fire, and I ended up sitting on James's chest in a hotel room in Sacramento, ignorantly, primitively trying to establish the upper hand for the eight-hour ride up to Eugene. Fran looked on. Things were going to change. Power and control. What had I gotten myself into?

I had been shocked while staying at home that summer when I changed the channel on the TV and my brother growled at me like some feral dog. Okay, I admit it was rude of me to change the channel, but good grief! The people I worked with at my group home work-study job in Eugene had way more severe disabilities and no-body communicated by growling.

"What would you think about James coming out to Eugene to live with Francis and me?" I asked my parents.

"Hey, Peg, did you hear that?" said Dad, with a nervous chuckle. "Thomas wants James to go to Oregon."

"Fine," said Mom, in her most stoic Irish manner.

Mom, you old softy. I know that game face. I don't think they really thought I was serious at first, and my offer just kind of hung there for quite a few days. Then they asked me, "How serious are you about this?"

Well, I was pretty serious. And seriously clueless as well. I hadn't given much thought to what a challenging change it would be for the folks. They loved the guy, and, whatever his challenges, they were used to having him around. But I had been thinking about it even before going back East the beginning of that summer. Serious enough that my super-literate friend Jay had loaned me a short story by Henry James, "The Pupil," a cautionary tale of responsibility and commitment and getting in too deep. I actually read it. But I thought, hey, we'll be in Eugene. You can't throw a rock without hitting a world-class behavior management expert. We'll figure it out.

But it was more than that. Since I had moved to Oregon in 1974, I don't think I phoned the family even once that James didn't ask in his idiosyncratic grammar, "When have I'm going to be moving to Oregon with you and Francis?" He wanted out. And once he got out, he never looked back.

In our Irish family of eight boys and two girls, I was number four, Francis was five, and James was six. We were a kind of distinct middle unit; always shared a bedroom in our cramped east Bronx housing project. Despite our protests and shamed by Mom's tears and our own guilt, Fran and I were often responsible for looking out for James. Working to overcome our embarrassment, we'd sometimes take him along to Mary's grocery store, the beach, or the park, and we'd stick up for him when Otis or some other clown told him to pull down his pants and sing the "Star Spangled Banner." After the fights that would inevitably ensue, Mom would always say to us, "Don't let them get to you. James doesn't understand that they're teasing him. He likes the attention. Sticks and stones may break my bones...."

And I had to admit, James always could carry a tune, even with his pants at his knees. Hey, he had it better than Jackie. That poor guy. If we ever felt bad about James, there was always Jackie to consider. We would see him walking with his mother around the Throggs Neck Projects—she seeming older, him smiling a toothy exaggerated grin, and goose-stepping stiffly frog-footed behind her. The other kids would all run away shrieking, "Jackie's coming! Jackie's coming!" Man, if there's a heaven somewhere, those two have front row reserved box seats.

* * *

When I left New York to move to Oregon, I was twenty-one and James was seventeen. By the summer of '81, he was twenty-four, and capable of taking a bus from Co-Op City in the northeast Bronx to the Pelham Bay Subway, catching the local train for a forty-minute ride to 125th St., switching to the express two levels down, riding that to 14th, walking across town to a sheltered workshop on the West Side, and doing it all in reverse going home in the afternoon. He's great at using transit systems and loves doing it. He got all the rope he needed from Mom and Dad to develop his independence that way. They were into family and community inclusion way ahead of their time. They rejected the recommendation to place James in an institution, helped start a parents' group in the Bronx, and worked to create opportunities for him.

They didn't have to worry too much about James learning his way around. He's always had that autistic memory thing going for him, and still does. He has precise videographic memories of events in his life, which he frequently plays back out loud. I'd love to record him and then get all his old special education teachers in one room to listen. They're all immortalized in verbatim neural movies, for better or worse: Mrs. Russo, Mr. Karen, Mr. Newman, and the others along with his friends. Some of the tapes are happy, but a bunch are about getting busted for hitting someone, cutting up, or what have you. Because he had that autistic behavior thing too.

James is severely patience-challenged, and has never suffered fools gladly. Tell him to quiet down once too often when he's talking to himself and you might want to duck. He was downgraded from "educably mentally retarded" to "trainably mentally retarded" pretty much after he hit early puberty, but it was just the behavior doing the talking. It still does. He likes his own space, likes to run his own show, and doesn't like it when anyone tries to deter him from his appointed rounds. I'm kind of hoping old age slows him down before he gets permanently banned from the buses or the library, but he's still going strong.

Mom likes to tell the story of how James would leave really early in the morning from the north Bronx to get to a workshop in lower Manhattan, even earlier than Dad did to get out to work. The whole behavior thing was in full gear at that point, and Dad would have to roust James out of bed with great difficulty, and, with this threat and that, get him out of the house on time.

One morning after the usual tussling, Dad had chased him down the stairs to the townhouse foyer. With one foot out the door, James turned around, looked up the stairs at the old man still in his underwear, said "Fuck you" as clear as day, and ran to the bus. Power and control. As the late tennis champion Arthur Ashe said, "Start where you are. Use what you have. Do what you can." It must be hard always being on the short end of the stick. You've got to pick your spots; use what you have. James picked a good spot that morning.

* * *

James is a lot different now. And a lot the same. Me too. He doesn't punch out windows when he's angry, and I don't ask him to eat airline peas, or do other arbitrary things he doesn't want to do. He still gets into trouble for occasionally pushing or bopping people who bug him, and earns extended breaks from the library, buses, or stores where these events occur. My fights on his behalf have moved from the Otises of the world to the systems in our community that just don't seem to get what cognitive disabilities are really about and what it takes to make an inclusive community for people with marginal behavior. This is all much more stressful for me than it is for him. He still has a wonderful head of fine brown and gray hair. Me, not so much.

I'm happy to say we've shared many pleasantly uneventful airline flights since that fateful first outing. He's even traveled on his own once or twice. He, Francis, and I shared a house for a while, then an apartment, another house, and then separate apartments in a duplex. I got my special education degree. Francis moved away and came back. I got married. Francis shared the duplex for a while, but he moved on, and James has been on his own now in that same duplex for almost fifteen years. He does okay, with a lot of support from us still, and a lot of burned microwave popcorn, but he manages. If future archeologists should by chance pick his apartment site to excavate, they'd likely conclude that people of our era in fact lived primarily on burnt microwave popcorn and frozen dinners. Sometimes I think he needs a change, more support, but it's not like there are lots of options out there, and I don't think he'd do well in a foster home or group home.

I do worry about his nutrition. One time after he got home from an independent grocery-shopping trip, I noticed that a package of pork chops was open and it didn't look quite full.

"James, where's the missing pork chop?"

"I ate it."

"Where?"

"On the bus."

Picture yourself sitting on a bus and the guy next to you starts gnawing and gnashing on a raw pork chop. To say he likes meat is like saying fish like water. He's a certified carnivorous maximus and knows the best butchers in town on a first name basis. Unfortunately, he doesn't play by all the food safety rules and he likes to create dining room sculptures consisting of pretty much all the leftovers in his refrigerator piled on one plate. I've got pictures of some them.

James gets a lot of understanding—and sometimes party invitations—from many of the young university students, artists, and natural food store workers who come and go in the larger ten-unit development that his duplex is in. Some new people don't understand why he feels compelled to deliver their mail from the box to their door, but the veteran neighbors fill them in and usually they're okay with it. Like the rest of the world, some are put off or fearful, and they stay that way.

I see James most every day and he comes over for dinner on Sundays. He likes eating my wife Janet's Italian cooking, and he likes being Uncle James to Sean and Ryan, our seven-year-old boys, sharing with them his love of the Three Stooges. You just haven't lived until you've watched the Stooges with James a few hundred times. I'm not kidding. We've had a lot of fun, and shared a lot of challenges. Every so often he'll come up and get his nose right up close to me and say, "Big Thomas" with a huge grin on his face. "Big Jim," I say in return. Francis actually gets more of those moments than I do. He's more of the brother and I'm more of the heavy, but it doesn't take too many of those to light up your world.

* * *

James is a computer guy. He maintains infinite lists of everything he'd like to buy, places he wants to go, things he wants to do, and, dead people he has known. We all need hobbies. He loves videos and viewing animated storybooks too, and has learned how to use a scanner to digitize photos. Technology is important to James and it's also brought about some major transformations in how I'm able to support him. If I don't have time to stop by his apartment, or he doesn't want me to bug him, I can drop in from home or work via computer to see how things are going. We also have a video link. But most important, James has played an important role in helping me to understand how the computers, sensors, and software used in home automation can help me do a better job of helping him. Let me explain.

Our venture in technology-based caregiving began one day about six or seven years or so ago when James wasn't feeling well. We went to the doctor, who asked some pretty typical questions. How is he sleeping? Is he getting up a lot at night? Is he using the bathroom more often? James isn't good at answering questions like that, and I told the doc that I didn't know either, because we didn't live together. Even if we did live together, I might not be able to answer accurately.

Not long after that, I became familiar with home automation systems and installed a network of motion sensors in his apartment. Thus began the process of learning how I could get more information about how James was getting along in his home. I didn't realize then how I would come to rely on these systems, and how profoundly it would change how I care for James and how he cares for himself. I've always been James's big brother. Now I was his Big Brother.

Scary, right? But it's funny how it's worked out. Something that looks at first glance as though it would be intrusive actually functions paradoxically to enhance independence. James likes having his own space and not having his pain-in-the-butt brother checking up on him in person all the time. I now have enormous peace of mind in knowing whether or not he's home at night, how he's sleeping, what kind of hours he's keeping, whether he's spending inordinate amounts of time in bed or in the bathroom, and whether he's carrying out key personal care routines like showering.

Maybe the biggest thing that's changed is that we don't fight so much about showers any more, because the system tells me when they happen. As noted at the beginning of this essay, as recently as a couple of years ago, our interactions around showers were a major source of tension. I had to make sure he took some every week, and he frequently resisted taking them. I think resisting showering served as an important way for him to assert control in his life, a behavioral tool he learned he could use long ago with our folks to compensate for being on the short end of the stick. Power and control. Use what you have.

Even cash incentives wouldn't do the trick because I never knew whether he had actually taken a shower unless I went to his apartment, and I couldn't always do that. For a while, he would actually honestly tell me whether or not he had taken one, and I'd pay him. Then he apparently had a head-smacking epiphany of some sort (Duh!) because he got way normal and always told me he had showered whether he really had or not, and I'd still pay him! When I found out the truth I'd often have to go to his house, and tell him that I wasn't going to leave until he took a shower, and that I might also eat all his potato chips if it took too long.

This routine changed when it became possible to have the sensors detect when showers had been taken and to have that information easily accessible via web page and email notification wherever I happened to be. Once I was able to know when showers really occurred, I could be consistent in working with James to earn cash or other incentives for taking regular showers. After a very short while, he "got" it. It has become now more of a straightforward, almost business-like affair and the tense, coercive element of the interaction has virtually been eliminated. But more than that, James has taken on more responsibility for taking showers without reminders and big payoffs from me.

We've come a long way, and the technology is powerful, but it's just a tool. Teaching and caregiving is still more than anything about relationships, a dance with a lot more footwork to figure out. I love the guy and I respect the hell out of him for trying to live his life the way he wants—even when it makes me crazy. We're both still learning as we go, and with luck we always will. But James no longer has to ask, "Who sings the shower song?" It's a tune he's learning to carry pretty well himself.

* * *

Tom Keating grew up in the Bronx, NY, and has lived for over thirty years in Eugene, Oregon, where he is Director of Eugene Research Institute, a nonprofit organization engaged in assistive technology research and development. His work focuses on cognitively accessible computing and design of systems for community living support, including creation of the Picture Planner™ icon-based personal organizer. Since 1981, Tom has been the primary caregiver for his brother James, who has autism, and this experience has been a crucial influence in shaping his technology development work and his understanding of disability. Tom is married and he and his wife, Janet, have twin seven-year-old boys who are the light of their lives. They enjoy running on the wonderful trails and paths in Eugene, camping and canoeing in Oregon's national forests and along the coast, and getting together for summertime extended family reunions at the New Jersey shore.

29.
My Sister, My Daughter

Maryjane Westra

When my parents brought my newborn sister home on March 26, 1962, Martha was a tiny five pounds and fit perfectly in my nine-year-old arms. It was the first time I had ever held a newborn and I walked around our home, rocking her gently and speaking to her softly. I made my sister many promises that night. I promised to help her with her hair and make-up the night of her senior prom. I promised to be the Maid of Honor at her wedding. I promised exciting activities for the dozens of children we were going to have. I promised to share deep, sisterly secrets. But most of all, I promised to love her deeply, passionately, and forever. The final promise is the only one I have been able to keep.

At the age of three, Martha talked and remembered amazing things like birthdays and all the verses to familiar Christmas carols. However, her language had an odd tone and her eyes had a strange piercing quality. She amused herself for hours by dangling strings or rocking rhythmically. She would fly into rages which lasted for hours, all because the furniture had been rearranged or Dad wasn't home for dinner. She refused to use the bathroom, except for certain select people. In public settings she was often out of control. Even though she appeared perfectly normal at birth, my sister developed autism and mental retardation.

When Martha was seven, in keeping with professional advice of the day, my parents placed her in a children's home—a euphemism for an institution. They felt she would thrive best if she was "with her own kind" and raised by professionals. I still remember the rows of beds in a sloped-ceiling, second floor of an old house in a run-down neighborhood of Rockford, Illinois. I was only sixteen, but I recall thinking that these professionals, however well-meaning, weren't able to control her outbursts and self-destructive behaviors any better than we could. Most of her time was spent with under-trained, poorly paid, albeit dedicated direct service workers. Staff turnover was high and routine and consistency were nearly impossible.

Martha was eventually placed in St. Coletta School in Jefferson, Wisconsin, where she lived her teen years, from 1974 to 1981. When she became an adult, services at St. Coletta ended. My parents sought an appropriate setting for Martha, but state-funded institutions were dreary and private institutions were expensive. I was a young adult, busy with a young family. I took Martha into my home, a dream of us together finally fulfilled. After missing most of her childhood, I painfully longed to be with my sister. At first my parents said the arrangement was temporary, but I convinced them to make it a permanent arrangement. They were reluctant because of the embarrassment of not being capable nor willing to care for her themselves.

Today, twenty-six years later, Martha continues to live with our family and work in a sheltered workshop. She was recently assigned a caregiver (better known as a Personal Care Attendant) to help with her daily cares. She still gets upset over changes in routine or when over-stimulated. She still dangles strings and still remembers birthdays, but she no longer rages and she uses the bathroom consistently.

Although I have always loved Martha passionately, she shows little affection. Her hugs are stiff and mechanical. Eye contact is strained and unfocused, not natural. Her life and activities are governed by comfort, consistency, and routine rather than any desire to please others. She taught me the meaning of unconditional love.

When I was a teen and young adult, I had recurring dreams about having a disabled daughter named Martha. Now, in my waking hours, I think of Martha more as my daughter than my sister. Growing up, my relationship with Martha was a source of tension for my parents and myself. They tried to protect me from over-responsibility for Martha's care and development. But I didn't want protection; I wanted to be included in Martha's life and the decisions around her care and treatment.

Siblings, especially older siblings, don't always need or want protection. The family—and especially the sibling with the disability—would be better served if there were mutual respect for the roles each member plays. For example, I was the primary caregiver for Martha when we were children. I was the only person Martha would respond to. She would let me do things for her that no one else could do, such as comb her hair and take her to the bathroom. She still wore diapers at the age of seven in every setting—except under my care. One time, when my mother was away from home due to illness, I took care of Martha for weeks without a single accident, even though she was not toilet trained. Clearly I was committed from a young age to taking care of Martha for the rest of her life.

* * *

Living with autism is simultaneously amusing and frustrating. My personal definition of autism is a total lack of common sense. Martha makes decisions and judgments based on training or observation, not on common sense. For example, she goes for a walk every day. This would seem like a healthy activity for someone who needs to work off frustrations of life. However, we live in Minnesota. I have seen her walk when the wind-chill is so low that exposed skin can get frostbitten in five minutes. I'm embarrassed to admit that one time she did experience frostbite under her chin when I wasn't paying attention and didn't realize she had gone out for her daily walk.

Martha's routine also dictates the clothes she wears. The change of seasons is hard for her. She will wear her winter parka—complete with lined mittens and face cover—on a seventy-five degree spring day. She wears the winter parka until I tell her it's time to switch to her spring jacket. However, I have to be careful not to make the switch too early in the season or she will be cold. The reverse happens in the fall. Change is hard for Martha.

Another no-common-sense habit is her practice of adding water to the dishwashing soap when it is nearing empty. Many of us were taught this method of extending dish soap, but Martha doesn't know when to stop. If I'm not paying attention, I will find her washing dishes with soap she has watered down until it is water so pure it could be poured in a glass and drunk without the taste of soap. I have learned to never buy clear dishwashing soap.

The list of Martha's habits is endless and they are such a part of our daily lives that our family accepts them without thought. For example, she was taught to shake hands and introduce herself when people come to the door. Her routine is to shake hands and introduce herself—always referring to herself in the third person. "She's Maryjane's sister," she'll say to visitors. She then asks, "Whacher name?" and asks for their birthdates, which she records in her vast memory bank of birthdays. Her birthday routine takes people by surprise and they often stumble if they are not accustomed to people with disabilities. In most cases, her routine for welcoming people is acceptable and somewhat amusing, but on occasion it is difficult. For example, when we host a large gathering with dozens of people coming to the door at one time, Martha's repetition is taxing, as it leaves people standing outside the front door.

Like many people with autism, Martha has routines that might strike some as a bit bizarre. One such activity is her personal walking route to work. Martha clearly missed the geometry class where students learn that the most direct route between two points is a straight line. She somehow devised a roundabout route to work that includes an exact path only she knows how to follow. She walks hundreds of yards opposite her destination, makes several sharp, military-type corners at precise points and then heads in the direction of her work.

Her path is so precise that I wouldn't be surprised to find a worn area in the pavement. At first I saw no harm in this practice, and thought it brought order and comfort to Martha. But people began to comment on it and even gather to watch the daily show. Their amusement at Martha's expense hurt and annoyed me.

* * *

There seems to be a myth that families with a disabled member pull together like the Three Musketeers. All for one and one for all and all that. People seem to think that families automatically focus selflessly on the member with the disability and reach well-thought-out decisions. While there are families that adapt well to the realities of a child's disability, there are many that do not. Most, however, fall somewhere in between. I don't believe my parents did well having a child with a disability, although many of their decisions were based on the wisdom of the day.

My parents, professionals themselves, believed the psychologists and medical doctors without question. Sometimes they took advice from childcare workers whose credentials were merely a huge dose of well-meaning. I can recall being told if we "make trouble," we risked losing Martha's home placement.

My family, like most families, tries to present our functional side to the public. When my parents talk to their friends about their children, they say that they decided to let Martha live with me. But when they talk to me, they accuse me of stealing Martha from them. There has been bitterness and disagreement about Martha's care, everything from whether she should drink alcohol (they say yes; I say no) or take medication for anxiety (they say no; I say yes), to how money should be spent on her care (they say she doesn't need much; I say she deserves to live the same middle-class standard of living as we do).

There are also disagreements about who should financially support Martha. I think my parents and brother should contribute; they think it's my total responsibility because I have chosen to be her guardian. There are issues about how Martha should be treated in my parents' estate. If my parents leave Martha money, her government benefits will be reduced. That's not a bad thing, since I'm not into shortchanging the government. But if my parents want to protect their assets, I feel that I should receive her share of the estate for past and future care as I have assumed total financial and physical care of Martha her entire adult life. My parents feel that because I chose to care for Martha, it wouldn't be fair to my brother to give me Martha's portion of the estate. My brother feels no responsibility toward Martha. He doesn't send cards or gifts or ask about her. In the end, it's their money and I have to live with whatever decision they make.

Martha influenced my decision to adopt children with disabilities. Regarding my son Jacob (who has profound disabilities), I have been confronted with the question, "Why would you adopt someone like that?" This question stops me in my tracks because the answer is so simple and clear to me, I can't believe someone felt the need to ask. (Answer: Because I can.) My husband and I were blessed with nine children through birth and adoption. All of them grew up alongside Martha. One bonus to having a large family that includes a member who has a disability is not needing to worry about long-term care. The only disagreement my children have (so far) is who will be the lucky one who gets Martha when my husband and I can no longer care for her. For the time being, she continues to do the dishes and I continue to love her and oversee her care.

Siblings mourn the disability, just like parents do. Living with a disability means grieving the loss of the dreamed-for child. I was sad when Martha should have started kindergarten. I lamented when she turned sixteen and didn't go to the senior prom. I sobbed at weddings, knowing I wouldn't keep the promise of being Martha's bridesmaid. I did, however, keep the promise of loving her—deeply, passionately, forever.

* * *

Maryjane Westra, the first-born daughter of a teacher and a preacher, is a graduate of Jane Addams School of Social Work at the University of Illinois–Chicago. She and her husband, Don, have nine children by birth and adoption. Maryjane is the guardian and caregiver of her sister, Martha, and is the executive director of an adoption agency. She enjoys educational travel, reading, gardening, sailing, swimming, singing (mostly in the shower), and playing Chopin on the piano. Maryjane especially enjoys challenging political powers and embarrassing her children and grandchildren.

30.
Getting from Then to Now

Susan Hamovitch

Recently, as I was placing a small bunch of bananas in my purse, I realized that it was finally time to sit down and write this essay. Well into middle age, I am most definitely an adult sib. Both of our parents are deceased and we have no other siblings. I'm it.

I didn't land here all at once, of course. Becoming exclusively responsible for Alan came gradually. And I didn't get here by myself. During each step in this journey, fellow adult sibs have provided me with help, advice, and validation.

For example, I used to think that the fact that Alan didn't speak, could barely communicate, and made weird noises was an unequivocal curse on our family. As cruel as it might sound, to me Alan was barely above a barnyard creature. My attitudes evolved, however, after I began to attend sibling gatherings. I was in my early thirties when my mother told me about a group that met at the local ARC each month. I didn't think about Alan often, and I certainly didn't think he'd had much of an effect on me. But I somehow I knew I had to attend the next scheduled meeting and every meeting after that. And so I did, solidly, for the next two years.

For the first couple of months, I sat in the circle the leaders had arranged, mutely astonished to hear other siblings describe their brothers and sisters in detail. I heard frustration, anger—and love. When I finally spoke, my voice choked on emotions I didn't know I had. I eventually whispered something about not thinking I had any issues. I soon recognized, however, that I had been profoundly affected by my brother, as well as by my family's and society's response to his disabilities. At the Christmas party that first year, I buried my head in the group leader's neck and wept

I gradually came to understand that although "weird" may sum up Alan in one neat word, it doesn't begin to describe him. I've come to realize he's a full human being, with strong opinions, a lively curiosity, a visual sensibility, and—I'll insist on it—a love of art. With startling clarity I've also come to realize I'd fight to the death for him.

But as I shoved the bananas into my new green leather shoulder bag, adding them to a sheaf of manila files documenting a three-year history of Alan's chewing and swallowing difficulties, I had to smile. A dozen ripe bananas was one of the "necessities" my family always packed on our monthly trips to see my brother. And, as always, Alan would polish them off in record time, punctuating the last swallow with a few high-pitched exclamations of pleasure, and a rapid twittering of fingers. He would descend with equal proficiency on the Mallomars.

Bananas and Mallomars invariably take me back to my earliest memories of Alan, when he lived in Letchworth Village, a now-closed state institution. In those numbing years, we fell into unvarying rituals that—like all rituals—serve complex psychological purposes. The picnics (which always took place in the privacy of the woods), the crumpling up of shopping bags, the dodging of bees, the brief hike deeper into the woods were all part of an unchangeable routine. I am sure these rituals gave us some stability and imparted a shadow of meaning to an absurd situation. But they also evoke a painful memory of a family that was stuck, that couldn't move beyond rituals.

There was a silence, a tacit refusal to talk openly about Alan or our feelings. This perhaps disturbed me the most, and, I now realize, created a crippling environment for all of us.

Thankfully, we no longer live in a social climate of denial and shame. But as my fellow siblings (who I'm now in touch with mostly over the Internet) have discussed endlessly, we have our own craziness to contend with. And sometimes this craziness is as daunting as the old days, or at least, hair-tearingly maddening. These days, I am most distressed by the bureaucratic obstacles that confront me and, of course, my brother.

Let me backtrack: In 1958, when their son was eight years old, and I was six, my parents piled Alan into their Chevy sedan, drove thirty miles to the hamlet of Thiells, and handed him over to the state. (I chronicle the effect this had on Alan and the family in my documentary film, *Without Apology*.) My father insisted that this momentous decision was largely my mother's. And I believe this was the case.

After thirty-three years in Letchworth (closed by a parent-led lawsuit), Alan moved into a spacious five-bedroom split level, a group home for eight men with 24/7 supervision by three teams of direct care staff. The group home was, we all agreed, overall a vast improvement for Alan.

My mother evinced her joy at Alan's move with the rebirth of a magnificent optimism. When Alan lived at Letchworth any hopes for her son had been quashed. It was thirty-three unchanging years for Alan, and herself. I caught sight of her new enthusiasm on her first, and, as it turns out, last, visit to Alan's new home. We picked him up at his house and drove to a picnic area nestled at the edge of a wood. Midway through lunch, she held up a banana, all the while looking intently at her son. "Ba" she said repeatedly. "Ba." After all these years, my mother's hope that Alan might develop beyond his limits was rekindled. He might actually speak!

After my mother died, my father was, quite honestly, lost. From that point on, he consulted me on every detail regarding Alan. I was grateful to be included, and so when I was forty, my father and I developed a kind of partnership, in which I was given some say over both major and minor decisions.

We traveled to Alan's group home together for regular visits and his biannual case review meetings. We began to question the medications prescribed to Alan (three different kinds of sedatives: Buspar, Serentil, and Risperdal) and I pushed for gradually reducing them. The team agreed to follow our requests, month after month, stepping down the dosage.

My father and I—who were so different in many ways—were in complete synch when it came to Alan's daily activities: we felt they should be meaningful to *Alan*, not to any of us, his family or his caregivers. Simple puzzles, which he enjoys, should be offered. My father, who loved outdoor sports, advocated for some of the same for his son. "He loves walking!" he would insist, with his characteristic impatience. The staff would shuffle, look at the conference table, as he'd demand, "Please, fergodssakes, take him on walks!" (And our response to their attempts to involve Alan in karaoke was the same: "You gotta be kidding.") Our repeated cries for walks and relevance fell, alas, on deaf, bureaucratic ears.

Then came one of the most difficult decisions I've ever had to make. Dad and I had both received a phone call from Alan's service coordinator. Alan had been recommended for a heart valve replacement—open-heart surgery. The choice wasn't as straightforward as it may seem. Although it was a lifesaving procedure, the potential pain of recuperation—which can last for more than a year—might be more than we'd want to subject Alan to.

Our first visit to a surgeon only complicated matters. He laughed at us. Alan couldn't be a candidate he insisted. No one would operate on Alan! Dad and I were wracked with indecision. I started a thread on the SibNet listserv and was relieved that no one would scold us if we ultimately decided that we didn't want to go through with the surgery—even if it meant a dramatically shorter life for Alan.

In the end, Alan had the operation, but under the knife of a pioneering team at NYU who had developed the minimally invasive, far less painful procedure that had only recently been introduced for this type of surgery.

I'll never forget the four days I was Alan's hospital companion. On the first night we were in his room, he took my hand and led me to the door. What did he want? Not about to deny him a thing before his operation, I followed ... apprehensively. Alan took to the corridors like someone preparing for a marathon. Together—to the horror of the nurses and the amazement of the mostly elderly men awaiting their open heart surgeries—we walked, no, we raced a half dozen laps around the ward, Alan's hospital gown billowing behind him.

The next morning, Alan sailed through the operation. And back in his room a few hours later, he spent the afternoon scrutinizing the watercolor that hung on the wall opposite his bed. It was a large, serene, semi-abstract composition with deep blues and purples which I too found beautiful. It was here that I learned that Alan can get lost in a painting, and he would drink it in every day of his stay for about twenty minutes at a time. And without question, my brother enjoyed his wheeled-in meals, wolfing down what for him was top-shelf cuisine with the bonus of a private room, butlers, nurses, and other doting staff. Within two days he was home, loping into his house, and flopping with the grunt of a world traveler into his armchair. His private smile suggested that he had thoroughly enjoyed his heart surgery.

After my father died, I promptly pursued legal guardianship. It came easily, there was no contest, but when the embossed-stamped papers arrived in the mail, I was surprised at the depth of my feeling. I wasn't this moved when I held my marriage certificate. I felt as though I'd been given something to treasure. A fellow sibling I'd met on SibNet echoed my sentiment—she too felt overwhelmed with emotion on receiving legal guardianship of her brother. We still can't quite understand why.

My saga as sole legal guardian has been fraught with more struggle than triumph, and I'm afraid much more conflict than I anticipated. My first act as guardian was to ask Alan's team to entirely eliminate his remaining small dose of sedatives. And, like most first acts upon assuming "office," mine were rebuffed. Earlier, I had had success rolling back Alan's prescription psychotropics. But then my father was at my side. Could it be that a sibling wields less clout than a parent?

I was taken to task by the staff psychologist, who insisted that if we eliminated the Risperdal entirely, Alan would undoubtedly become more agitated, a major obstacle to inclusive programming. Most notably, I was told movie attendance would be a thing of the past. Movie attendance? I didn't care if Alan saw the latest Tom Hanks feature!

I won't venture onto the thin ice of describing "who" Alan is, but I've become convinced that Alan's mystery forms the basis of our relationship. I am humbled by being in Alan's presence, as I interpret and reinterpret my sense of what he's experiencing, whether he's enjoying himself at any moment, or what's causing his occasional, apparent cries of distress. I'm acutely aware that I can hardly ever answer these questions.

I profoundly wish that my devotion to guessing what makes Alan tick could be wed to the practical and protective care provided by Alan's team. I'll tell his team of Alan's fascination with all kinds of shapes and objects. I'll suggest that he's got an artist's sensibility. (You can't avoid projecting our world and vocations onto him.) They look uncomprehendingly at me as I tell them about the things I know he thoroughly enjoys. "I've seen him stare at an original watercolor! His face relaxes, and his eyes focus." "He loves the feeling of a sewing machine vibrating beneath his hand." "Why must Alan always be in large congregate settings—movie theaters, auditoriums, stadiums, and other places in which he doesn't seem particularly interested—in order to be considered integrated into mainstream society?" Can't a person be involved in some solitary pursuit, and still be a fully normalized individual?

But because we couldn't agree on the big picture, it's not surprising that we wouldn't agree on the "small" things, like medication and food consistency, as well as my brother's daily program. I found myself begging. I asked the psychologist, the nurse, team leader, and head psychiatrist to approve the reduction of the last 5 mg of Risperdal. Repeatedly rebuffed, I appealed to the assistant director and felt a wave of relief any family member will recognize upon meeting a fair-minded, knowledgeable administrator. He informed me that, as legal guardian, I had the ultimate authority over psychotropic medications.

And so it was done. Alan's sedatives were promptly eliminated and within six months, he'd found his old equilibrium. I felt we'd triumphed. But my elation wasn't shared. Indeed, Alan's team and I had become adversaries. And to my dismay, they took what I thought was a dramatic step. Because of Alan's initial increased vocalizing (and admittedly, Alan's constant noise through those first few months was quite irritating) they deemed it wise to put his meals in a blender. Meat, vegetables, pasta, toast, salad, all would have the same ground consistency with no plan for a change. The reason? His increased vocalizations might cause him to choke.

My ally in the administration, the one who advised me on the rights of a legal guardian regarding psychotropic medications, suggested that a written prescription from an M.D. cannot be argued with.

I stashed the three ripe bananas in my purse and made my way to Dr. S., an internist, who I hoped would issue such a prescription. My husband, Al, a well-behaved Alan, Alan's service coordinator, and I gathered in his office. I opened up a thick folder, removing the latest speech therapist's report. Convinced by the data, Dr. S. agreed to write the prescription for solid food. I hadn't achieved my goal yet, but I thought—I hoped—I was a giant step closer.

After our meeting, the three of us bee-lined to our favorite Mexican restaurant. This is now where we go when we visit Alan. It's almost—dare I say—a ritual. The situation is not exactly easy, and I can understand why my parents chose Harriman State Park for our meals. As the owner greets us warmly, I worry about whether Alan's oddly contorted expression and his fluttering fingers will be accepted, or whether the other diners will shoot us dark looks of annoyance, or worse…disgust. I notice with relief that the restaurant is almost empty as the owner ushers the three of us to a booth.

I watch Alan tuck into his chicken molé. He obeys my directions to take it "slow, Alan, slow." When I ask him, with a bit of a stern edge to my voice, to chew, he pouts, sets his fork down—and he chews. After his meal (much of it, alas, splattered down his shirtfront) my brother focuses his attention elsewhere—and he's quiet! I follow his gaze. With rapt fascination, Alan is watching the waiters pass from the dining room through the swinging doors to the kitchen, and then reappear.

Postscript: Alan's team refused to accept the recommendations of the speech therapist and Doctor S. As of this writing, Alan's diet has been subjected to pureeing, and gum problems have resulted. Because of this and other perceived failings in his care, I am in the process of researching alternative residences for my brother.

* * *

Susan Hamovitch *is an independent filmmaker and teacher. Her most recent documentary,* Without Apology, *is a personal saga about her brother who has multiple intellectual disabilities (www.withoutapology.com). The film has screened nationally and internationally, winning Best Feature documentary award at the Brooklyn Arts Council International Film Festival and Second Place Audience Award at the Hearts and Minds Film Festival. She is currently working on* Mama Sue's Garden, *a film about the aftermath of Hurricane Katrina (www.mamasuesgarden.com). A work-in-progress version screened at the New Orleans Human Rights Watch Film Festival (April, 2008). Susan lives in Brooklyn with her husband and two Catahoula dogs and teaches documentary studies at The New School University.*

31.
Finding Molly

Jeff Daly

For forty-six years I heard a soft voice in the back of my head saying *Molly—Molly*—with little realization why it was there. Molly disappeared when she was three years old and I was six. And now there she is, waiting to touch me again, but she is fifty years old. The little voice is still there but it is coming out of my mouth. "Molly—Molly Daly, it's me—Jeff—I am your brother and I'm so sorry it took me so long to find you."

When you hear stories of brothers and sisters long separated by adoption or other family issues, the siblings often resemble one another in mannerisms and physical appearance. What I found in Molly was a sister that I had no memory of—until I saw her face. Flashes of images filed away long ago filled my head. Molly looked just like our mother, and, more surprisingly, like the Molly I knew all those years ago. Molly studied me for a few moments and took my hands to her face—and accepted me back into her life.

In 1957 our parents followed doctor's advice and sent Molly to Fairview, a Salem, Oregon state institution "for the feeble-minded."

At that time she was deemed profoundly retarded and our parents were told it would be best for Molly and the entire family if she was sent to a place where she would receive proper care. This confused little brother was left behind and repeatedly asked where my sister had gone and why she went away. When I did, I was sent to my room, so I soon learned not to ask about her. Molly became a distant memory.

The family lore was that Molly was a "vegetable" and would never know anyone. Almost fifty years later I reunited with my sister, who I found was now living in a group home only an hour away from my home. Instantly, I knew the tales told were not only incomplete but completely wrong. Molly was a whole person with intelligence, wants, needs, and emotions, just like me. But unlike me, she spent her first three years in our home and was then dropped off at an institution, where she would spend the next thirty-six years of her life.

When the institution closed Molly moved into a group home, where she lived for ten years before I found her. Like Rip Van Winkle awaking after decades of sleep, Molly awoke to a new setting that was radically different from what she had known. At Fairview, Molly grew up with thousands of other rejected children who received little individual care or education. For months, I researched state records to learn more about Molly's life. The details were painful to read. Daily activities I took for granted as a child were missing from her life.

At her group home, Molly was excited to watch food being prepared and to sit and eat off a plate at a kitchen table instead of a tray in a cafeteria. She reveled in having her own room with a door she could close and a closet with her own clothes that did not have to be shared. Molly was not a "vegetable" and yet had lived all those years away from her family, deprived of the things I took for granted. I felt an overwhelming sense of anger, regret, grief, and most of all guilt. All I could say to her was, "I'm so sorry, Molly." I was sorry I had not challenged my parents and found Molly years before. I regretted that I hadn't discussed Molly's condition with my parents before they died, and, most of all, I was sorry that I hadn't had a sister all those years to share family activities with.

Regrets quickly gave way to joy as we began to spend time together. Over the next several months, Molly and I learned how to effectively communicate and to reestablish a relationship that skipped more than four decades. Molly awakened to family and has reveled in it. She wants everyone she meets to hug and kiss her and says so with clearly stated words. She learns new words every time we're together and has no problem remembering them the next time we meet. I believe that had Molly been provided the opportunities I had, her life would be entirely different. What was missing was a loving family environment with social interaction. The guilt I felt was erased with a plan of action I devised to give Molly what she had missed for the previous forty-seven years.

I am fifty-six years old and find I often revert to acting like a child with my sister, wanting to continue from the point when we were separated. Molly loves the outdoors and when she says "water," I pick up the hose and Molly screams with glee when I squirt her bare feet. She enjoys car rides, especially when she is able to sail her arm out the window to feel the wind blow through her fingers. Rather than being transported in a wheelchair accessible van, Molly rides with me in the family car and our trips are full of adventure, laughter, and travel.

On one outing, we returned to Fairview, the institution where Molly spent her childhood, as well as to Astoria, Oregon, where she lived with our family for three years and where I spent my adolescence. As we spent hours walking and talking, Molly learned about me and I learned about her. She was not afraid visiting the institution that had since closed. In fact, she was quite angry with me when I said I thought it time we end our first visit there, and only a guarantee of an ice cream cone convinced her it was time to leave. In Astoria, we walked the streets she should have walked with me in childhood and we visited our old family home. We talked about our parents and the mistake they made so long ago and the lesson of forgiveness.

Molly has worked through the emotions I felt, too: anger and grief. As we first became reacquainted, Molly displayed her anger by turning away, pushing my hands away when I touched her, or simply refusing to communicate. I would sit with her and say "I know you're angry that I didn't find you sooner and I'm sorry. We should have been together as children but we're together now and I promise to make up for lost time." With time, she greeted me with open arms and accepted my promises. She's at peace with the brother who finally returned.

Now into our fourth year together, Molly and I have a solid brother-sister relationship. We don't see each other every week, but I stay close enough to assure her I am now a permanent part of her life. I continue to tell her stories about our parents, a brother she hasn't met, and the excursions I have planned. She now enjoys music therapy and through it is better able to express herself. I am always thinking of new experiences for Molly and we repeat the activities she enjoys the most—having her hair styled, shopping for her own clothes, going for a walk on the beach—activities most of us take for granted but experiences in a new lifestyle a family provides.

That little voice whispering to me now comes directly from Molly's mouth. Rip Van Winkle returned to a society that had changed, and thankfully, so did Molly. Molly, unfortunately, did not sleep through the very difficult early years of her life and the best we can do is learn from the mistakes of the past. We hope and pray that the practice of segregation and isolation of those with disabilities will be a distant memory never to be repeated.

* * *

Jeff Daly is president of SFO Productions, based in San Francisco, California. For more than twenty-five years, Jeff has filmed news and sporting events worldwide including the Olympic Games, the Super Bowl, and 60 Minutes segments. Jeff is the recipient of a 1999 Peabody Award for his contributions to ESPN SPORTSCENTURY and has won two Emmys. In 2007, Jeff and his wife, Cindy, produced Where's Molly, a feature-length documentary based on his life story of finding his sister after a nearly fifty-year separation. In a series of interviews with family friends and professionals, Jeff explores his parents' decision to give up their young daughter and examines the emotional impact of such an action. The film provides a historical look at how the State of Oregon processed the thousands of children given to the state for protection and care. To learn more about Jeff's film and to read about other families who searched for lost family members, visit www.wheresmolly.net.

32.
A Family Affair

Jeff Moyer

At 11 a.m., the Thanksgiving table was only set for four. When I had called my brother an hour earlier, he had declared—in no uncertain terms—that he didn't want to join us for Thanksgiving. I considered calling again. Maybe he really wanted to come for the annual feast. Mark can change his mind in a flash and perhaps I could loosen his resolve. On the other hand, I didn't want to risk the trauma of sending my son and his girlfriend to get Mark only to have him change his mind again halfway across town or, worse yet, during Thanksgiving dinner. Both had happened before.

I was conflicted, but my commitment to Mark's inclusion in family life got the best of me. I asked Donna if we could reset the table with Mark's place restored, and even add another place setting if needed. Maybe his caregiver would want to come too; that way Mark could stay as long as he wanted, and leave when he chose, under his own power. My dear Donna showed her usual calm and flexible nature and I picked up the phone to explore Mark's current state of mind and his caregiver's willingness to drive over and join us for dinner.

In agrarian times, an individual with a cognitive disability could live supported by an extended family that would, as a collective, attend to his or her support and care. My own grandparents moved to Cleveland from North Carolina in 1918, where they each had twelve siblings living within walking distance. The upheaval of the industrial revolution caused many nuclear families like my grandparents' to move to cities seeking work in factories. That dislocation shredded the natural web of familial, supporting community.

As work took fathers and others away from home, the responsibility for individuals with cognitive disabilities shifted to fewer and fewer family members—and eventually, to the state. The draconian state institutions established in the late nineteenth century and their unreformed existence until late in the twentieth century forced the remanding of many a son and daughter into a lifetime of institutional misery. So it was for my younger brother and for my family.

In 1962, Mark was an eight-year-old with a severe cognitive disability. His life was shackled with the restraints of no hope of education nor safety from increasingly fierce attacks by neighborhood children. Our family stewed in a witch's brew of unacceptable circumstances, closed options, mounting strain, and looming dread and uncertainty. John Kennedy was president and his administration brought the plight of individuals with cognitive disabilities into the public consciousness. His own sister, Rosemary, lived in a reportedly lovely private institution half a continent away from the Kennedy family. Meanwhile, in 1963, my little brother, Mark, was sentenced to a barren institutional prison in the rural outskirts of Columbus, Ohio—150 miles from his home in Cleveland.

When I was a child, my mother told me that she didn't want Mark to be a burden to my sister Bonnie or me when we got older. Doctors had advised that institutionalizing Mark would allow a regular life for the family's other children. But instead, Mark's institutionalization created a wrenching circumstance that grounded our lives in pathos.

Prior to moving west in 1968, I was a full-fledged member of Mark's family support team. But during my fourteen years in California, Mom, Dad, and one grandmother attended to Mark's needs.

I made annual visits to Ohio and would see Mark without fail, although my visits provided scant support. During one particularly dark visit—following Mark's attempt to run away at age sixteen—I swore that I would some day find a way to give him a real life. Regardless, institutions were the only options available at the time—and an awful option in many ways. My working class parents were required to pay the highest level of the institution's sliding scale for my brother's upkeep. It certainly wasn't care. Mark suffered horribly during the nineteen years of his incarceration at the Columbus State Institution for the Mentally Retarded.

Then, in 1981, because of my family's advocacy, Mark was moved. He was transferred to a smaller but still-brutal place, a bleak, ancient, staff-housing barracks on the grounds of a state institution in Cleveland. The open sore on my heart that had festered during my years apart finally forced me to immerse myself in Mark's circle of support. With my wife and six-year-old son, I moved back to Cleveland in 1982. Mark lived forty-five minutes away and it required a full-court family press for me to visit him. I am a person who is blind, and that necessitates a partner who is willing to drive. But more than my wife's engagement as a driver was required; we were a family, so our kids came along too. Our children became part of Mark's life and he a part of theirs.

My wife and I shared responsibilities for Mark with Mom, who lived nearby and had remarried following Dad's death in 1980. Mom was Mark's guardian, but I was his advocate. The facility where Mark lived was run by a for-profit provider that rented the moribund buildings from the county. The large facilities were considered progressive, boasting buildings that housed fewer than twenty people—still bad, but far better than the fifty-bed wards in an institution housing thousands where Mark had languished for nearly two decades.

The new facility was run like a non-essential service organization. Family involvement wasn't encouraged, it was required. The facility closed over the long Thanksgiving and Christmas breaks. Families were told when to pick up their cognitively disabled members and when they could return them after the three-night shut-down. So at Thanksgiving and during winter holidays, Mark would be our house guest—and Mark's overnight visits required total, full-time involvement. I had added Easter and his birthday to the overnight calendar.

When Mark slept over, I would become ragged with sleep deprivation. I couldn't sleep for more than the brief periods between Mark's forays into the night seeking cigarettes and coffee. So during his quarterly overnight visits, I would stay up with him throughout his waking hours and during his sleep-disturbing night walks. It was stressful for everyone.

Mark's personal heaven would include an inexhaustible supply of cigarettes and coffee or cola. Consequently, there was a constant need to regulate and supervise Mark's smoking during visits. But Mark was sly in satisfying his tobacco addiction. He had smoked since he was eleven, when his institution introduced cigarettes as a means of control. When he visited, I rationed his cigarettes. During one Christmas visit I groggily awoke to the heavy smell of cigarette smoke. Mark had padded past my bedroom, slipped below my hair-trigger radar, and obtained the pack of cigarettes I had hidden. By the time I found Mark in the kitchen, he was smoking his fourteenth cigarette.

During another Christmas visit, Mark arrived at our home with a corncob pipe and tobacco. I told Mark he could smoke in the basement, where I thought he would be safe and where the smoke would not bother anyone else. I set him up with a large glass ashtray on top of the washing machine on a concrete floor. While fiercely smoking his pipe, Mark must have knocked a burning clump of tobacco onto the rubber-gasketed edge of the top-loading door. It was enough to start the washing machine's plastic interior and load of still-dry clothes on fire. Mark hurried upstairs and reported the fire, which was put out by the local fire department.

In 1992, my first marriage ended after nineteen years. Like all divorces, multiple factors in our lives combined to create the critical mass. While not the "cause," the impact of our ongoing commitment to Mark was one of the factors. Life is different for those who marry into a family where someone has a severe disability. Invariably a level of commitment is required that produces stresses and strain over time.

As a blood relative, one has an unswerving duty. For in-laws, however, the extra responsibility of caring for a sibling with a disability affects the total fabric of the relationship. When resilient relationships are nurtured by the support of an extended family, such stresses can be absorbed—the immediate family need not bear the full weight of the care alone. But without natural family supports, the emotional strain can be considerable.

After my divorce, I lived in an apartment and arranged holiday visits for Mark without my family's help. Mom and I had shared overnight responsibilities for years, but gradually I took it all on, since her second husband had suffered burn-out caring for Mark. After Mom's death in 1995, I became Mark's guardian. And, with that new authority, I advocated for improvements in Mark's living situation.

I was successful in moving Mark into an eight-bed group home in inner Cleveland. Then, with the help of my second wife, I was able to launch him into supported living. Thus began weekly visits, attending to ongoing guardianship responsibilities, and anticipating all of my brother's needs. After several intermediate moves, I finally moved Mark into an even better place. I rented a small home where Mark lived for several years with one other man and support. Mark lived within walking distance of me in his own happy home. I acted as the super and I provided or arranged and paid for all house and yard maintenance. But I didn't—couldn't—do it alone.

Here's just one example of the involvement required by my mate to help me support my brother: One Sunday evening near midnight the phone rang. An almost hysterical direct care provider told me that the toilet in Mark's house had overflowed. Armed with a plunger, my wife and I drove the few blocks to Mark's house and we were able to resolve the messy problem. But there is no simple formula for maintaining this sort of resilience and selfless patience. My second marriage also ended after a decade; it too was stressed by the commitment we had made to Mark's support. However, I am forever in my second wife's debt. Without her unflagging assistance, I would not have been able to secure Mark the home where he receives high-quality, supportive care.

Since then, the parts of my life concerning Mark have stayed much the same. Donna, my dear life partner, visits Mark with me every week and prepares holiday meals to welcome my brother to our small family gathering. My son, now an adult, also always joins us at these events. He loves his Uncle Mark, treats him with deep respect, and provides transportation as needed. In our little clan, Bonnie—Mark's and my sister—and my darling daughter live across the country.

Commitment to providing this level of support can be taxing. We have found that humor is a great lubricant and resilience is not just a quality, it's a necessity. As significant as the demands are, real circles of support can also provide for tender and genuine moments of generosity, love, sweetness, and joyful celebrations.

My children have learned lessons of humble acceptance from my brother. They've also learned that Mark is wise and that wisdom is not a subset of intelligence. Mark's wisdom can be seen in his forgiveness, his love of service to others, his generosity and courtesy, and his compassion. He seeks opportunities to give generously and offers an openhanded trust. I have seen him offer to give away a beloved birthday gift when a care provider complimented him about his new possession.

Mark's true gifts—which he offers everyone in the family—are love, a simplicity of spirit, an abiding appreciation of small gestures, and the gift of time. However, we've learned that a gentle and patient nature is a prerequisite before Mark's gifts can be received. We've seen that if we're impatient or unable to engage Mark selflessly, we'll only experience frustration.

Research has disclosed the polarized nature of participation by adult siblings of adults with cognitive disabilities. We tend to be very involved—or very uninvolved. Today's gold standard of care for people with cognitive disabilities is supported living, and by definition, family support is essential, albeit complex. One doesn't just commit themselves to support a sibling when one has a family—for better or worse, it is a family affair.

As the Baby Boom generation's parents are aging and dying, we siblings will bear the mantle of guardians and advocates. This is an entirely new element in the social contract, one that will demand communal effort, requiring contributions, time, and talent from everyone in the family—as well as friends, volunteers, and professional service providers.

The mobility limitations of my blindness have forced a greater involvement from my family than would otherwise be required. I am proud that I have been able to pull Mark up the housing food chain from brutal institution to a quiet suburban supported living home. But it would not have been possible without the support of every member of my family. In addition to my own family, those who truly care for my brother include the broad circle of caregivers who have become quasi-family members to Mark. Our definition of family is broadening, and, as a sibling, I am grateful for everyone in Mark's circle who cares and supports him.

In the end, Mark changed his mind about Thanksgiving. He and his caregiver drove to our home and joined our family circle. As the six of us gave thanks and celebrated together, I was reminded once again that love and support—for any of us—is a family affair.

* * *

Jeff Moyer was born in 1949 in Cleveland, Ohio, and began to lose his vision at age five due to a rare progressive retinal condition. That same year, Jeff's brother Mark was born with a severe cognitive disability. The impact of Jeff's progressive blindness and his brother's life circumstances gave Jeff a powerful understanding about the need for social change to improve the opportunities for, and inclusion of, people with disabilities. Jeff received a Master's in Rehabilitation Administration from University of San Francisco and in 1992 began work full time as a consultant, author, songwriter, publisher, and motivational speaker. Jeff has presented at numerous conferences and has spoken and sung in forty-seven states and internationally. He's been featured on The CBS Evening News, 20/20, *the BBC, and as a commentator on NPR. Jeff has two adult children and has been successful in moving his brother, Mark, back into the community with supported living services. Jeff's original music and books are available at www.jeffmoyer.com.*

33.
Life with Jay: An Interrupted Family Journey

Carol Lynstad

I grew up in a household bursting with eight family members, and, at any given time, an assortment of dogs, cats, hamsters, rabbits, and goldfish. In many ways, it was the kind of life Norman Rockwell depicted during a simpler time in America—filled with family camping trips, vacations to Grandma's, days at the beach, and grade school playfields. My brothers were in Little League and my sisters and I were active in Girl Scouts. Our neighborhood rang with the sounds of childhood games of tag and kickball. Family life in my childhood home was subdued only by the presence of my brother's disability.

As Jay's younger sister by two years, I gradually became aware that the rest of the world considered him as "special" in ways that didn't appear to be positive. Despite this, Jay was still my first playmate—the one who taught me fun bathtub games and how to get to the cookies in the kitchen. As I grew into adolescence, Jay's behavior and appearance certainly caused me some heart-stopping, cheek-burning moments, but all in all, sharing childhood with Jay did not pose many personal challenges to me.

I have come to realize that other members of my family had more troublesome responses to his disability—perhaps most of all our parents. For my mother, having her second child diagnosed with mental retardation as a toddler appears to have been the beginning of a life lived with anxiety, sadness—and eventually—episodes of depression. Our father, who approached all areas of life in a reasonable, logical fashion, responded by setting out to "fix" the problem of Jay. His time became increasing devoted to seeking the services of professionals and engaging in the activities of the newly-forming parent advocacy organizations. I've realized that it was my parents' reaction to Jay's disability—not my brother himself—that has had the most long-lasting impact on my personal development. It has led me at times to respond to the world around me in uncomfortable and unhealthy ways.

Jay died very suddenly in mid-life, predeceasing our parents. His death left a gaping hole in our family identity. Although he had moved out of the family home and into a local group home, his routines and life still very much defined our mother's daily life, which in turn rippled through the rest of our relationships with her and him. How were we now supposed to move into the future? I had been orchestrating my life to fit my future role as Jay's primary guardian—something my husband had embraced as well.

Jay's death came as we were shifting our focus to the needs of our aging parents. Their health needs had forced us to rally to help them sell the family home and relocate across the country to be near children who could provide support. With Jay now gone, our mother's fragile hold on emotional stability was more obvious as she slipped into bouts of depression and painful expressions of rage. As we, her adult children, circled the wagons and compared memories of our family life, we came to realize that it was she, not Jay, whose well-being we were always desperately tending to. Even as young children, we sensed our mother's joyless approach to life and tried not to add to her worries.

Led by our father's example, we colluded through unspoken agreement to always do what we hoped would make her happy, or at least ease her load. We also learned early on to hone our antennae to the needs of others—a lifelong habit which we all have practiced on each other as well as the people who came into our lives as adults. The plight of one of us sends reverberations of anxiety through the rest. Several of us—myself included—have followed our mother into the netherworld of depression and anxiety. Unlike her, due to greater societal acceptance of mental health problems, we have sought medical and therapeutic treatment. Still, worry and anxiety are constant companions—only eased when family members appear to be doing OK.

So—is this Jay's legacy—a family credo of angst? It needn't have been. Jay is remembered by his family as a man who found much pleasure in life. He had a well-developed sense of humor and took great joy in his favorite possessions, outings, and well-iced cups of Coke and a Big Mac. He frequently took us with him down a path of silliness and taught us to laugh at the absurd. Perhaps if our parents had been able to enjoy life along with him—and had not felt as burdened about the existence of his limitations—the rest of us would have followed suit and felt less need for hyper-vigilance.

Here, then, is my wish for all siblings of people with special needs: I wish their parents will find the resources needed either within themselves—or by reaching out—so they and their families can recognize and experience the joys of life. Jay would surely approve.

* * *

Carol Lynstad grew up in New York State and has lived in New York City and the Midwest. For the past twenty-five years, Carol has worked with people with disabilities and their brothers and sisters in many capacities. She has been an ardent advocate for adult siblings for many years. A devoted naturalist, Carol enjoys visiting wildlife sanctuaries whenever time permits. She and her husband, the artist and playwright Robert Giordano, now live in western Washington State.

34.
The Hidden Brother

Allan B. Goldstein

Following our parents' deaths from cancer, I never questioned becoming the guardian of my younger brother Fred, a person with intellectual disabilities. But at the age of forty-nine, I did question whether I could again be a brother.

As a young adult and independent of my family, I had deliberately distanced myself from Fred and only heard about his activities or saw him at family gatherings. My need for distance was a reaction to too many Sunday visits to Fred at his institutional home of sixteen years—the Willowbrook State School for the Mentally Retarded. Memories of these years of visits still shake me; still, I can't accept the lost time that could have been directed at Fred's development. In the fifties, the importance of providing a stimulating home environment for kids with disabilities was something our parents didn't know about. Nobody knew. With a dearth of services and hope for Fred's future, Mom's and Dad's feelings of guilt and inadequacy fueled frequent fights, especially after they delivered their four-year-old child to Willowbrook. We *all* lived in turmoil.

Ironically, these myriad visits, coupled with memories of sharing a bedroom until Fred went away, embedded my devotion to my brother. How many times did Fred balance himself on the teething rail of his crib giggling and looking at me before toppling to the linoleum floor for Dad to rush in to pick him up? Giggle—clunk—cry—Dad. Often!

I've never wanted to believe that Fred has defined my life, but he has, and in significant ways. I didn't have children with my first wife, claiming it would take away time from seeking work as an actor. But I also recognized that my marriage resembled my parents' and feared completely losing my wife to the child. My second wife and I decided that at our late stage in life we'd rather devote time to each other. But the bottom line is: Because of my experience with Fred, I never needed to be a father.

Although I'm not my "brother's keeper"—he lives in a group home and participates in a day habilitation program—I am now his avid advocate.

As an advocate, I've experienced the ferocity of never-had schoolyard battles. For instance, the supervisor at Fred's former residence insisted that his gastroenterologist knew our family's history of colon cancer but still didn't want to see Fred for a biennial colonoscopy. I found this odd and called the doctor, who, as it turned out, hadn't heard of our family's history with the disease. The procedure was scheduled immediately and performed a second time ten days after the first to confirm that all seriously advanced polyps had been removed.

The staff at Fred's day program wouldn't support his newly stated desire to learn to read and write, saying, "We don't bother when they reach that age." Yet studies show that IQ can improve at any age, and that a student's ability to learn isn't as important as a teacher's ability to teach.

And finally, his residence counselors refused to act on his repeated requests to move from his group home of twenty years. Perhaps they had become possessive of my brother, unable to "see" him and his unhappiness.

"What's that?" I asked a counselor, about the screaming coming over the phone.

"That's your brother. Sometimes the guys get like that, and we just let 'em go."

But when Fred began refusing to shave, brush his teeth, get haircuts, I knew his anti-social behavior indicated anger or depression.

"It's his choice," counselors said. With deinstitutionalization, a person with intellectual disabilities was no longer *told* what to do but asked what he *wanted* to do. Their philosophy was influenced by the work of Swedish "normalization" pioneers Bengt Nirje and Niels Erik Bank-Mikkelsen, who discovered that, if asked, people with intellectual and developmental disabilities have opinions about how to spend their day, their year, their life. Fred's counselors relied on this philosophy as a convenience to avoid conflict—if he didn't want to brush his teeth, so be it—apparently unaware that people with intellectual disabilities sometimes died young because plaque from their teeth clogged their arteries and caused heart attacks. As it is, several of my brother's teeth have rotted and been extracted.

Ultimately, Fred and I found other agencies—one providing a sensitively staffed, peaceful residence that often exudes the aroma of good home-cooking, and another offering a challenging day habilitation program that supplies computer time, speech training, and meaningful work. He is now a student of numbers and letters; his level has improved from *severe* to *moderate* mental retardation. *Everyone* can learn!

Currently, we have discussions on the street, in my house, in the theater waiting for the movie to start on Truly Important topics such as: "You can't tell every girl she's your girlfriend". . . "You have to let the dentist clean your teeth". . . "What do you mean you can't take your own shower? You're not a baby!"

I often forget Fred is different, especially since his sociability invites attention, particularly from women.

"Fred asked me to marry him," said Martha, a former day program participant with Down syndrome who always unwrapped his lunch and laid out his paper napkin. "He got down on one knee. My sister says I should ask for a ring."

"Did you get down on one knee?" I asked Fred.

"Yes," he said.

Where did he learn to do that? Did he know what marriage meant? Did he understand sex? This led to interviews with social workers, and the discovery that Fred wasn't interested.

Nonetheless, proposals of marriage come teasingly from mature women who don't have intellectual disabilities—they fall for Fred's charm and kindness. But at a ballgame, a teenage girl sitting in front of us stared at my brother as the rest of us cheered each announced player. She stared…and stared. At his crooked eyeglasses? At his droopy left eye? Another time, while on the corner of a busy intersection, two young girls gawked at Fred. "Bahhhh," said Fred, waving his hands at the girls as if in a horror film, sending them away. And yet that same day, two twenty-something women "cruised" the two of us, making me think of what could have been had it not been for a premature birth and forceps squeezed too tightly around my brother's head.

I initiated a Best Buddies chapter at the college where I once taught to establish friendships between people with and without intellectual disabilities. The BB regional director invited Fred and me to present our story at the annual International Leadership Conference. We did it again two years later and then accepted similar engagements at nearby colleges. I don't know where Fred learned to bow, but he appropriately acknowledged the raucous applause after each presentation. I also don't know why he is so comfortable on airplanes. But I do know that documenting our relationship since Mom's death has me now seeking a publisher for our book.

At Fred's last semiannual evaluation, his counselors asked me to select a date because he had saved money from his day program jobs to take my wife and me to dinner. This was from a guy who has never learned to say thank you, who has never bothered to remember counselors' names (maybe because in the past, staff rarely remained long), and who has always insisted that others do for him ("Here," he'll say, handing me his coat). Now he is successfully earning money, exulting in the independence promoted in his new home and daily routine.

Recently, a planned visit was delayed by several days. We finally connected at a deli counter where we sat, facing the street, sharing a roast beef sandwich. As we watched people walk by, Fred said, "I was worried about you."

"I'm fine," I said, stunned by an interest that I had only fantasized about years earlier when becoming his guardian. "We just returned from vacation, so we got busy. I'm fine. Thank you for worrying about me."

Perhaps my promoting his individuality has permitted both of us to develop.

I'm not surprised that Fred tells everyone about me—I'm his connection to typical life.

And Fred isn't surprised I tell everyone about him—maybe he always knew that I could again be a brother.

* * *

Allan B. Goldstein *is an instructor of English at the Polytechnic Institute of NYU in Brooklyn, New York, where he teaches writing to students of English as a Second Language. His interest in his work is a result of experiencing Fred's communication difficulties and exclusion from society. Allan retired from two decades of professional acting when he realized he could "work" every day as a personal experience/memoir writer. His essays appear on the e-zine "Mr. Beller's Neighborhood" and he is currently seeking representation for his book,* Finding Fred. *He and his wife, Phyllis, are avid open water swimmers and take vacations wherever there are excellent swimming conditions. They train year-round as U.S. Masters swimmers in New York City and live by the East River in the Yorkville section of Manhattan. Allan is grateful for Fred's permission to share their story.*

35.
Transition

Ann P. Kaiser

My brother Jim was born in 1950. He was a premature baby, the smallest one who had survived up to that time in central Kansas. When Jim was growing up, no one could tell our parents exactly why he was fragile, late to walk, and never really learned to talk. All our parents were told was that these things sometimes happened to premature babies.

When Jim was eight years old, the Dominican nuns at St. Rose Hospital opened a special school for children with disabilities who could not be admitted to public schools. My mom drove him twenty-two miles every day so that he could have speech therapy and four hours of school. His progress was very slow.

Living in a small town with our parents was a quiet, sweet life for the most part. Jim rode his bike all around our town with its single stoplight. Everyone looked out for him and kept my mother informed of his whereabouts. There was a small network of families with children with disabilities that moved together through special schools to sheltered workshops, to weekly bowling and holiday parties. All of these children lived at home with their parents. And, everyone expected they would always live there.

After my father died in 1973, my brother continued to live at home and attended a day program. Life was much as it had always been. Then, in the early 1990s, my mother's health became increasingly fragile. My sister and I were concerned about both her ability to care for my brother, who had multiple health needs, and the potential trauma for both of them if my brother were to move to a group home. There were no good choices. Eventually, my sister found an agency in the county where she lived that could provide a supported apartment where Jim could have a full-time live-in caregiver and a roommate

The transition that we had dreaded for so long was difficult. But, the transformation in my brother that followed was amazing to all of us. In a few weeks, he had made his first male friend, his roommate Matthew. Matthew teased Jim and he liked it. The two of them had wordless jokes involving snorting and laughing that no one else understood. Jim wanted clothes like Matthew's (jeans and sneakers, t-shirts with sports heroes on them). No more baggy pants and buttoned shirts! With new clothes, Jim found a new attitude. His speech became a little clearer. He looked at people and he responded when asked direct questions, instead of turning away and hiding his face.

My relationship with my brother changed when Jim left home. Somehow, he became a person in his own right, and was no longer just my brother still living with Mom. We had a relationship, just the two of us. Because I lived 600 miles away, much of our new relationship involved weekly phone calls.

I have told many people the story of Jim's transition to living in a supported apartment, recounting how he blossomed after he left home. For me, recounting that story is a way of saying to families who are understandably afraid of transition that there is so much to be gained for everyone when a person with a disability moves to a home of his own.

I wrote the two poems that follow during the year after Jim moved into his first home away from our parents' home. These poems are snapshots of our lives in transition.

As an adult, my brother was diagnosed with autism spectrum disorder. He died in 2005.

On Hearing Your Voice on the Telephone

I could not have imagined your voice
If I had ever thought to imagine it

In my mind you were silent
All these years
A silence deeper than being wordless

Once when you were three
I watched you sitting in a red wagon
Alone in the driveway
Waiting for someone to take you for a ride
It was hot, we were wearing sunsuits
I was small and brown

I stood in the front door
Watching, detached, already fading away from you
As if I were drowning at sea
And you were floating on the surface
I could not reach you
If I had cried out
You would not have heard
Your eyes unseeing, vacant
I would have drowned without your notice

I wondered what you were watching
Or hearing
That gave rise to your worried look
I knew it was not me

Now your quiet voice
Six hundred miles away is a silk prayer flag
Waving in the mountain wind

I am stilled by its curious soft sound
Where does the wind come from?

Conversations with My Brother

I call every Sunday night
Between seven and eight
His roommate or his housemother answers
My brother comes to the phone
When he is called
"It's your sister . . ."

He does not say hello
He has only recently learned to talk
On the phone
I hear his heavy breathing
Helen tells him
"Say hello...Say hello, Jim."

I say "Hello, how are you?"
A conversation of questions
That can be answered yes or no
Winds its way through a long ten minutes
I cannot tell when he is telling me his truth
Often I cannot understand what he is saying

"Did Helen take you shopping for new pants?"
"Did you buy jeans?"
"Uh huh"
"What color are they?"
" 'een"
"Green? Are they green?"
Surely not

He tells me he is going home
That is so clear
 "Home...ma...ma...home."
I don't know what to say
I know he is homesick

I do not know if this is the week
He will go home to visit

I tell him I love him
"I think about you all the time"
"Here is a big hug, can you feel it?"
I ask to talk to Helen
Sometimes I have to ask several times
I cannot tell if he wants to keep talking
I don't want to stop talking if he still has something to say

I ask Helen how his week was
"Is there anything he needs?"
"Anything I can do?"
In her practiced way, she tells me just
The good things, professional reassurance
Our decision was right
"He is doing fine."
"He is feeling a little more like himself."

When I hang up
I am filled with unnamed sadness
Our Sunday night conversation closes the week
With a hollow sound
Leaving a dark draft of loneliness
In the room as I turn out the light.

* * *

Ann P. Kaiser is the Susan W. Gray Professor of Education and
Human Development at Peabody College of Vanderbilt University
and the Director of the Vanderbilt Kennedy Center's Family Research
Program. She's also the director of the National Sibling Research
Consortium. Ann is the author of more than 130 articles and chapters
on early interventions for young children with disabilities and
children growing up in poverty. She has received numerous awards

for her research and mentoring including the Harvey Branscomb Distinguished Professorship at Vanderbilt University. Ann grew up in central Kansas with her brother, Jim, who had significant intellectual disabilities and autism. In addition to her professional interests, Ann is a poet and paper maker.

36.
Growing Up and Growing with Harold

Carolyn Graff

Our family was the only family in our town who had a child with cerebral palsy. And I was the only child I knew who had a brother who could not walk or talk. In some respects, that made me—and our family—pretty special. We were definitely different. Most of the time, being different was not a bad thing.

Our spacious old home was surrounded by huge oak and pecan trees and like every home in our neighborhood, it sat on an acre of land. Our yard and house was popular with the kids in our neighborhood. There were snacks in our kitchen and the huge trees were great for climbing.

All the kids knew Harold. They knew him as the boy who sat at the window or the large porch that spanned the front of our house. As kids ran inside for snacks, they'd run past Harold, who was usually sitting in his wheelchair or lying in his bed. Once one of my friends asked me, "Why doesn't your brother walk and talk?" I answered as matter-of-factly as I could, "He can't. He just doesn't walk or talk." That seemed to do the trick and away we ran to play.

Of all the kids in our neighborhood, my friend Nancy knew Harold best. She was curious and asked questions about him. Unlike other kids, she'd walk right up to Harold and speak to him. Since his responses included only a turn of his head or a glance in her direction, even Nancy did not talk to Harold very long. Waiting for Harold to respond was not easy.

For the most part, Harold was easygoing and everyone who came to our house seemed to like him. However, because he didn't speak or even show signs of recognizing one person more than another, hanging around Harold was not very exciting for most of my friends. And if kids were loud or rambunctious near him, Harold would sometimes become upset and try to cover his ears. He'd drop his head down and pull his wrists up to cover his ears. And if he was really upset, he'd try to bite his wrist. On those occasions, I moved our activities to another part of our house or outside.

When my friends seemed interested in Harold, I helped them get a smile and laugh from him. I knew that by speaking his name in a low tone followed by "ba-ba-ba-ba-ba," Harold would usually smile and sometimes laugh. So, I helped people do that. This was fun for my friends, Harold, and me.

Just as I knew when my friends felt uncomfortable around Harold, I also knew that some adults who visited our home were uncomfortable around him. A notable exception was Mrs. Palmer. She lived next door to us and was one of my favorite people. Earlier in her life, she had a stroke that left her with a slight speech problem. When she visited, she walked directly to Harold and talked to him. And when she did, her speech problem was hardly noticeable. Harold loved her visits and smiled for long periods as she chatted with him in her coarse and husky voice. I decided that Harold liked her deep voice and her pleasant manner and he knew she liked him. I loved the fact that Mrs. Palmer felt comfortable around Harold and that he smiled and laughed when she talked to him.

Other people in our neighborhood—and many relatives—did not appreciate Harold as a person. He was not a visible part of our community. Born in 1951, Harold did not attend public school, or any school at all, for that matter. He did not play with other kids in our neighborhood, take walks, go on picnics, read books at the library, go swimming, or attend church. When we went to the library, Harold sat in the car with my aunt. When we went to the park or zoo, he sat in the shade away from the noisy children and animals. When we went to the ocean for a summer vacation, Harold sat at the edge of the ocean so he could feel the waves washing over his legs. In short, opportunities for others, particularly adults, to get to know Harold were limited.

There were times that Harold's differentness bothered me. One of those occasions was on a trip my sister Judy and I took with my mother and Harold by train to visit my grandmother and relatives in Montana. My mother held and carried Harold during the three-day trip from Georgia to Montana and on the return trip to Georgia. Harold cried a lot while we were on the train. I decided he did not like the loud noises of the train. My sister and I sat in a seat across the aisle from my mother and Harold. I curled up in my seat and hoped that Harold would stop crying. Sometimes he was quiet for short periods of time, but then he started crying again. I was so relieved when that trip was over because he seemed so unhappy and there was nothing I could do to help him.

When I was twelve, my family went camping in the north Georgia mountains. We loved to sleep in our huge tent, cook over a campfire, and take hikes. After our family set up camp, a group of Boy Scouts arrived and set up their tents in the adjacent camp site. The boys stared endlessly at Harold and our family. I considered walking over to explain Harold's cerebral palsy to them, but, at twelve, I felt awkward and different. Unlike during my younger years when being different was fun, being different at twelve was a real problem for me.

Harold continued living with my parents into his adulthood. He was very healthy and only needed medications for a seizure disorder. But in June 2001, at age forty-nine, Harold began losing weight and refusing to eat. Judy and I and our sister Barbara immediately became concerned about possible gastroesophageal reflux disease. The physician who examined Harold did not agree with us, however. My mother was very worried. My father had died seven years earlier and was not there to support her. Judy, Barbara, and my brother, Roger, attended to Harold's daily care—a responsibility previously assumed by our mother. We supported our mother emotionally as best we could and avoided making decisions that our mother believed were hers to make. We gingerly intervened on Harold's behalf only when necessary.

That summer, I was completing my doctoral program at the University of Kansas. I was scheduled to defend my dissertation on August 24th, Harold's fiftieth birthday. Throughout the summer, I flew from Kansas to Georgia to spend as many weekends as I could with Harold and my family. I tried to give my sisters, brother, and mother needed respite, and to comfort Harold and let him know I was there for him.

Then, in August, Harold was hospitalized after two months of difficulty eating and ongoing weight loss. Diagnostic testing showed that he had unusual and complex architecture of his stomach, small intestine, and left lung. As we had suspected, he also had severe gastroesophageal reflux disease. The only treatment was a surgical procedure that would require placing Harold on a ventilator for a long period of time—and possibly the remainder of his life.

While I was staying with Harold in the hospital, the surgeon discussed Harold's condition and the proposed surgical procedure with me. He asked my opinion about the pending surgery and I told him that our family had to discuss it and make the best possible decision we could for Harold. I knew my answer but could not speak it. I then looked at Harold, nearby in his hospital bed. He seemed to have an opinion too. He was asking for no more intervention. The tubes going into his body bothered him immensely and the sedating effects of the pain medication prevented him from using the senses and abilities he had to be aware of his environment. I knew a tracheostomy and ventilator would be very difficult for him. He wanted to go home.

I flew back to Kansas that Sunday evening so I could prepare to defend my dissertation. My mother and siblings agreed that Harold should not undergo the surgery. He was discharged from the hospital and we all agreed to care for him at my mother's home—Harold's home.

On Tuesday, my sister Barbara phoned to tell me that the minister from my family's church had baptized Harold earlier that evening. My mother had been concerned about Harold's inability to attend and enjoy church services throughout his childhood and adulthood. The minister came to my mother's home and baptized Harold in the Methodist tradition. Barbara told me that after the baptism, Harold relaxed and was peaceful. Our mother was pleased. Two hours later, Harold died.

The news of my brother's death devastated me. I felt sad for my family and selfishly concerned about myself. I called my brother and asked if the funeral could be postponed until Saturday. I told him how important my dissertation defense was to me. Roger, who was working with the funeral home and minister on the arrangements for Harold's funeral, said, "We can't wait, Carolyn. We need to get this over with. We are all so tired." I understood. I told Roger I would arrive in Atlanta on the following day and attend Harold's funeral on Thursday. During the turbulent flight home, I reflected on my life with Harold. I was to give the eulogy at Harold's funeral. And the topic of my dissertation, which I would defend the following day, was intervention with siblings of children who have chronic illnesses and developmental disabilities. The irony was not lost on me.

The next morning, I called my dissertation advisor and told her about my brother's death. I assured her that I would return to Kansas on Thursday evening and defend my dissertation on Friday. I packed my bag and sat down to write a eulogy for my brother. The minister had asked for a family member to speak at the funeral service. No one in my family wanted to do this. The only way I could speak in front of my dissertation committee, I decided, was to also speak at Harold's funeral. I knew I could do this for my family and for Harold.

My flight from Kansas City to Atlanta for Harold's funeral required a stop at Chicago's O'Hare airport. Once inside O'Hare, a dark cloud and a severe thunderstorm settled over the airport and stopped all planes from departing and most planes from arriving. I called Roger to tell him about my delayed arrival time and sat back to watch the heavy rain and lightning and listen to the strong wind and loud thunder. I felt sad and numb. I thought of my dear brother

Harold and immediately connected the lightning and thunder with him. I "saw" him running around the dark skies, creating such havoc and causing this thunderstorm. Because Harold had spent his entire life in a wheelchair or in bed, it made me smile to think that he was now free and tearing across the skies and heavens. Thor, the Norse god of thunder and war, also came to my mind. I decided that maybe Thor was in his chariot following behind Harold as they both raced around the heavens having a great time. I felt numb and knew that fatigue was taking its toll on me.

The storm passed and I boarded the plane for Atlanta. From my window seat, I watched the thunderstorm recede in the distance as the plane headed south; I smiled at the thought of Harold's freedom. My brother and his wife met me in Atlanta at 1:00 a.m. on Thursday morning. Harold's funeral went like clockwork. We arrived at the church at 2:00 p.m. and found the church filled with relatives, friends, and neighbors.

The time arrived in the service for me to speak about Harold. I took my two pages of typed notes and a beautiful tribute my husband had written and began to read. As I relaxed, I looked up and saw tears in the eyes of everyone in the church. I was overcome with emotion. What an incredible experience this was for all of us. I started shaking, then composed myself and returned to reading the eulogies. As I neared the end of my readings, a young man with Down syndrome stood up from the pew. He spoke about what a wonderful person Harold was and how much he would be missed. People began to cry. I finished my comments and sat down. The service ended and my family and I were ushered out of the church. My family headed for Harold's burial at the cemetery. I headed for my rental car and drove back to Atlanta. I arrived in Kansas City late Thursday evening.

At 10:00 a.m. the following day, I began my dissertation defense. My friends and my husband observed as I presented an overview of my study of siblings and answered the committee members' questions. As stressful as the day was, I felt Harold's reassuring presence as I spoke to my committee. After all, I would never have chosen this topic if it wasn't for him. Here I was, the day after his funeral, and on his fiftieth birthday. The committee congratulated me on successfully completing my dissertation defense. One committee member, unaware of my brother's death or his birthday, commented that I seemed to be glowing. I smiled and knew that Harold was right there with me. It was an honor to share this moment with him.

* * *

Carolyn Graff *shares her life with her husband, Paul, who lives in Leawood, Kansas, and her work experiences with the University of Tennessee Health Science Center in Memphis. She is an associate professor in the College of Nursing, Chief of Nursing at the Boling Center for Developmental Disabilities, and director of the Ph.D. program in nursing. Her entry into professional work with children with developmental disabilities and their families began in 1980 when she coordinated services for children with disabilities in western South Dakota. Since that initial experience, most of her professional work and interests have focused on children and adults with developmental disabilities. She frequently visits her mother and siblings, who live in northeast Georgia, and her husband's family, who live throughout the United States. Besides spending time with her husband and family, she enjoys early morning walks along the Mississippi River, hiking in the Black Hills of South Dakota, bicycling anywhere, reading, and gardening.*

37.
Easier? No...The Issues Just Change!

M. Doreen Croser

It was a cold winter night on eastern Long Island and a bitter wind was howling against the cedar shingles of my small cottage in Westhampton. A crackling fire burned in the fireplace and I was comfortably settled in my favorite wing chair reading a mystery novel. Quietly, my brother John came over to my chair, propped his arms on the top, and leaned over. "Doreen?" he asked somberly, "When you gonna retire?"

I looked up and said, "I don't know, John, maybe in two or three years. Why do you want to know?"

"Just wondering," John replied as he stumbled back across the room, settled in his chair, and began channel surfing.

Several weeks later we were together again. As I was making supper, John marched into the kitchen and announced with a big smile, "Doreen, I make up my mind. I gonna retire in two or three years."

I looked at him and burst out laughing. "And what do you think you are going to do then?" I asked. "You are too young to retire. You are only fifty-four!"

Of course, I really knew what was on his mind. John may have a significant intellectual disability but as the saying goes, "there are no flies on him." He was letting me know that when I retire he wants to come to live with me in Westhampton. I smiled at his gleeful face and not-so-subtle approach. I told him that we would talk about it when the time comes. It was much too soon to "worry over"—to use one of John's favorite phrases. But, of course, I have been "worrying over" John's future for a very, very long time.

Who could blame John for wanting to live with me in our hometown? While I had moved out into the wider world to pursue a career, he had stayed in Westhampton, where he lived with my mother during the first forty-seven years of his life.

In Westhampton, he had the stability of friends, connections, places to go, and things to do. He was part of a real community. Everyone knew him and watched out for him. He was a well-known personality who bicycled around town on a bright red three-wheeler given to him by the local volunteer fire department. And even now, when we go out to a restaurant, shopping, or to a concert, people come up to John and ask him how he is doing and where he has been. I am constantly amazed by how many people care about him and how he cares about them. Clearly, he benefited from living in a small town where people knew each other as youngsters and continued to support one another over the course of their lives.

But, like so many people with disabilities whose lives are turned upside down when their parents or caregiver dies, John's life dramatically changed when our mother died at age 70.

Mom had been diagnosed with ovarian cancer twenty months earlier and decided she wanted no treatment. Her decision was devastating to all six of her children, but it was especially devastating to me—I had battled breast cancer—and to my younger sister Carol, who was in her sixth year of fighting ovarian cancer.

We wanted our mother to "fight" but she just told us in her gentle, matter-of-fact way that she was older and not as strong as we were. "Besides," she said, "my parents, my younger sister, my other relatives, and all my best friends are now gone. I have lived a good life." Our mother possessed an enviable inner peace and a great faith that brought comfort to her in her final months. But that didn't make it any easier for those who watched her slowly waste away—especially for my brother John.

John was affected most by our mother's illness and subsequent death. He lived with her and was there every day to help. He cut the grass, went to the store, and ran errands. He was also there to see her slipping away.

Mother never told John that she had cancer and was dying. I thought her decision was totally wrong. When I pleaded for her to tell him, she said, "He can see that I'm ill and that I'm not getting better. He doesn't need to know that I have cancer. He will only worry."

Worry?! John repeatedly asked, "Will Mom get better?" I was truthful and told him "no," but I did not go against my mother's wishes until the day she died.

I will never forget the look of horror on John's face when I told him that she had cancer. He just looked at me and said, "Cancer—oh nooooo!" At that moment, I promised myself that I would never keep such important information from him. He had a right to know when his loved ones were terminally ill. Like everyone else in the family, he needed to have the chance to help out, make peace, be supportive, grieve, and say goodbye.

Our mom died at home late on a Saturday evening during Memorial Day weekend. With a heavy heart, I trudged up to John's room to give him the news. As I sat on his bed and told him she was gone, he pulled the covers over his head, let out a pitiful moan, and said, "Oh no, what I gonna do without my mother?" What indeed?? Understandably, John was very angry, anxious, and depressed over my mother's death for a long time. In fact, I think his mourning period stretched into several years. And why not? His whole life was turned upside down.

The family had discussed John's future with Mom before her death, and, of course, we had also discussed it with John. His co-operation would be absolutely essential to the success of any plan. While our mother would have preferred for John to live with me or our sister Ritamary, that was not what John wanted to do. He made it very clear that he did not want to leave eastern Long Island and he definitely did not want to live with me since I was just too bossy. Furthermore, I was living in Maryland and he did not want to move to Maryland, nor did he want to live with any of his other brothers or sisters who were residing in various east coast states.

Fortunately, years earlier when my father died, John had been placed on a waiting list for residential services. So, upon my mother's death, I called the New York State Office of Mental Retardation & Developmental Disabilities and asked them where he would be placed. Of course, there were no group home vacancies.

After a month with me, John was placed temporarily in a ten-person group home on the north shore of eastern Long Island. He lived there for more than a year and then moved into a smaller home with three roommates. The good news was that his new residence had many amenities. John had his own room, it was in a decent neighborhood, and it had a swimming pool and many modern conveniences. The bad news was that it was thirty-eight miles from his hometown. John had no friends either in the home or the suburban neighborhood, and there was no town within walking or bicycling distance. He was socially and physically isolated.

John has been in this group home now for about five years now and his adjustment has been a mixed success. As in most community residential programs, the staff turnover has been constant. Since John has always had difficulty with changes in his personal environment, he does test the limits of new staff, most of whom are much younger than he is.

On most days he gets along with his roommates, but conflict is not unusual, and, periodically, his behavior can be challenging. When he acts out, I call to warn him that if he doesn't straighten up and apologize for being so mean, I will not be picking him up for the weekend. Usually, he calls me the next day to say, "Doreen…I make up with everybody. I say I sorry…you come get me?"

I've noticed that he seems to have the most difficulty getting along with his roommates—and everyone else—in the late fall. I think he suffers from a seasonal depression disorder that exacerbates his behavioral outbursts. He hates winter and his mood sinks as the daylight grows shorter. I've shared this observation with John's group home staff. They like John and try their best to work with him and be supportive despite his outbursts.

I have come to appreciate how little control my brother has over his life and how difficult and frustrating it must be to be so dependent upon others for all his daily activities. When he lived with my mother, John had a great deal of choice, freedom, and independence. Now he has to fit in to the rhythm of the group when traveling, doing errands, going to a day program, or just socializing. Because John can be very self-centered, it must be a constant struggle to adjust to the needs of three roommates and staff and to be reasonably considerate of others.

Currently, John is tolerating suburban group home living, but I can tell he is clearly dissatisfied with his life. He wants to return to his hometown and is quite vocal about letting everyone know that he wants to move *soon*. Every time he sees the president of the agency that oversees his group home, John asks him when his new Westhampton home will be ready. The president tells him that he is working on it but it will take time...he is on "the list." Evidently, things are not happening fast enough for John, so now he has developed another strategy—he will just come to live with me when I retire.

More than anything, I want to support my brother in having a more satisfying quality of life. He wants to be in his hometown surrounded by people who care about him and I believe this is very reasonable and should happen. I also believe that family members should support one another, and, thankfully, that belief is shared by my sister Ritamary, who is also involved in John's life despite living more than 500 miles away.

The seemingly simple solution would be just to have John move in with me when I retire, which is on the horizon—although he doesn't know that yet. But, unfortunately, fate has not been kind to me, and my golden years are not turning out as I had hoped.

I was happily looking forward to returning to my beautiful hometown, spending time at the ocean, and volunteering at the performing arts center and nature preserve. But now, for the second time in my life, I am dealing with cancer. So far I am holding my own, but it is too soon to tell if I will survive another year or two, or, hopefully, many years.

Dealing with cancer, making healthcare choices, articulating my final wishes, and planning for the last months of life were decisions that I was able to make without much hesitation. I knew what I wanted to do and I knew what needed to be done. So, I just took care of business and put my affairs in order.

But when it comes to doing the right thing for and with my brother, I am very conflicted and continue to struggle with a variety of issues, especially surrounding his living arrangements. As the oldest sibling, I have always been involved in my brother's life and I am extremely concerned about who will serve as his advocate if I am no longer there to help. This will be especially problematic if he continues to stay in his current residential placement. With no family or friends nearby, who will determine that "all is well" or step in if he needs help?

I also worry about the fact that if John does come to live with me he would lose his residential "slot," and a placement in Westhampton would never be an option. Although a more creative housing option might be possible, at this stage, I really don't know what that might be.

On the other hand, assuming my health stays reasonably stable, perhaps John should just come to live with me and we can enjoy whatever time we have together. I wonder if we would both be happier having a shorter but more satisfying time in our hometown?

It troubles me to know that if he does come to live with me and my time ends up being short, his life will again be in absolute turmoil. He has already told me repeatedly that he would "not be happy over" anything happening to me. His words "not be happy over" translate to sadness, grief, and many, many tears.

John, Ritamary, and I have talked about all these issues on many occasions, as we try to pave the way for a future that strives for a better quality of life for John and peace of mind for each of us. John now understands that Ritamary will be stepping in to help him when I am gone and he is happy about that. The seed has also been planted that he should think about going to live with Ritamary in Virginia. While he wasn't willing to move in the past, he is getting older and he seems to appreciate being with his family as often as possible.

And so the debate continues to rage in my head and John continues to talk about moving in with me. Thankfully, no decisions are necessary at this very moment. We will continue to think about our choices and to talk about what would be best. Although the path is not yet clear, in my heart I know that we will eventually make good decisions because we love one another and care about each other's well-being.

I also know that we are very fortunate. We have several options and choices, while too many men and women with disabilities have no options and no one who cares about them.

As I reflect on the challenges that John and I have faced over the decades, I can remember asking my mother if life got any easier as we got older. "No," she had said, "the issues just change." I remember those words now as I struggle with how best to support my brother. It seems to me that the decisions we face as our time on earth grows short are the most challenging and heart-wrenching, especially if a beloved brother with disabilities will be left behind.

* * *

Doreen Croser became interested in developmental disabilities many years ago when her younger brother John was diagnosed with multiple disabilities including mental retardation. Since that time, she has served in numerous professional and volunteer capacities while remaining actively involved in John's life. Doreen is the first woman Executive Director of the American Association on Intellectual and Developmental Disabilities (formerly AAMR). Established in 1876, the AAIDD is concerned about improving the quality of life for individuals with developmental disabilities and their families through research, education, training, and public policy initiatives. Doreen loves to sail and lives on Maryland's Chesapeake Bay with her precious pup, Gretta. Gretta is fourteen years old but thinks she is a puppy, and on most Friday nights she and Doreen drive up to Eastern Long Island to spend the weekend with John. When Doreen retires, Westhampton will, again, become her permanent home, as it was when she was a child.

38.
Forty Years Is a Long Time to Wait

Kitty Porterfield

I was forty-five years old when I first heard the words "sibling" and "special needs" in the same sentence. My mother happened on an article, which she sent to me, about siblings of children with disabilities. I was stunned by what I read. I had always assumed that what I had experienced and what I had felt about my childhood were my own problems. It had never occurred to me that other brothers and sisters could have felt the same way.

I located the author of the piece and called her—an uncharacteristically bold move for me. We must have talked for an hour about her work and what she had learned in her research on young siblings of children with disabilities. I couldn't hear enough. A huge, dark curtain was being raised on a window in my life, and the sunshine that came pouring in was blinding.

After our conversation, I searched for everything about sibling relationships that I could find—which wasn't much in those days. I discovered Sibshops, the creative peer support groups for school-age sibs, and attended a training conference for Sibshop facilitators, run by Don Meyer, the editor of the book you are holding. I traveled from my home in Virginia to Chapel Hill, N.C., to sit in the front row and listen to Don's stories. Finally, I was hearing about people like me. I laughed and cried my way through the day.

At Don's invitation, I shared some of my own experiences with the parents, teachers, and social workers who were there. For the first time, I was telling *my* story.

At the demonstration Sibshop that followed, I watched the young boys and girls chasing balloons, eating pizza, and sharing stories about their sibs. I envied them the chance to express the rage and sadness and loneliness, as well as the love and pride, that they were experiencing in their attempts to be normal children in sometimes very difficult situations. I envied them the feeling of having some place to belong. My parents would have taken me to a Sibshop, if there had been one. It's not that they didn't try, but in those days there was no wisdom about the impact of a disability on brothers and sisters, no vocabulary with which to have the conversation.

Back home in Virginia after the conference, I read more and more, and I began to write about my own experiences growing up as Johnny's sister. Having already spent two years working with a therapist trying to sort out my family and my life, I now embarked on another long journey pouring my stories into the keyboard and onto the page. I began to speak to parent and professional groups about my experiences, each time opening new windows and letting in more light.

Johnny is my younger brother. He was born with cerebral palsy and intellectual disabilities. We were two kids growing up with two parents in a stable, loving, middle-class home in Pennsylvania. Except that we were a very different family. Back in those days—I was born in 1941 and Johnny was born in 1944—no one knew much about disabilities. The veterans hadn't yet come back from the war. Rehabilitation was not yet a big industry. You didn't see many wheelchairs on the street. There was no Public Law 94-142 (the predecessor of today's IDEA). My parents had to drive to Baltimore twice a year to visit a doctor who knew what cerebral palsy was and how to treat it.

As a kid, Johnny had leg braces and walked with an awkward gait. His speech was not easy to understand. He laughed appropriately, but sometimes very loudly. People stared at us on the street. Other kids called Johnny a "retard." But our parents were determined to take Johnny wherever we went, and our family was pretty much on display all the time we were growing up. It was very uncomfortable for me.

Johnny's medical appointments and his therapies took time. My parents' concern was focused first on his survival and then on his growth and development. ("Just put him in an institution," the doctors told them. "He'll be better off there.") My mother followed the research, interviewed doctors, and continued to look for new answers. She managed all of Johnny's therapies.

At the same time, my dad went, with another father, to the local school board to petition for public classes for students with disabilities. They succeeded, and at age seven, Johnny was able to start school. As Johnny grew older, Dad devoted his efforts to leading the community in building a medical center and sheltered workshop to provide services for Johnny and other young men and women like him.

In the midst of all this industry, it was hard for me not to feel left out or left behind. Johnny and I remained good friends, but I became a pretty angry sib. Today, I sometimes meet parents who—on hearing my story and my plea for more support for young sibs—say to me, "I am so glad that our Danny doesn't feel that way. He loves his brother. He always smiles. He is no trouble at all."

I smiled too. Through the long waits in the doctors' offices, through the uncomfortable restaurant meals when people stared, through the walks home from school that seemed interminable because Johnny moved so slowly—through it all, I smiled. I knew that my parents were carrying a heavy load. I knew how sad they were about Johnny's challenges. I didn't want to make their life harder, so I smiled. They never knew—until much, much later—how much I hurt too.

In recent years, I have come to see that—aside from being born to parents—having Johnny for a brother was the single most defining influence of my childhood. His birth with disabilities, to which the whole family had to adapt, was like a tornado blowing through our house. It changed everything and everyone. And I have spent the years since being overwhelmed by, angry at, working around, growing with, and rejoicing in his life.

I have also learned that we were among the lucky ones. We have had the resources to provide Johnny with the support he needed. My parents had the education and the skill to advocate on his behalf. We have been surrounded with a loving family and good friends. And from the very beginning, Johnny has been the kind of guy that other people like to be around.

But still *I* had to wait forty years to get the support and information that I so desperately needed.

Johnny has had a great career. He remains a bright, caring, funny fellow. He attended school until he was eighteen, although he remains functionally illiterate. Since then he has had steady jobs at sheltered workshops, first in Scranton, and then in Rochester, New York, where mother moved after our dad died. When Johnny retired in 2002, his colleagues gave him a big retirement party. He is much beloved wherever he goes.

But now, retired, sixty-four, and a tad portly, Johnny is one of the first generation of special-needs kids to live long enough to become an aging, special-needs boomer. Johnny lives in assisted housing. Because his balance is no longer stable and stairs are a hazard, he recently moved to a new, one-floor home. Mother, a hearty ninety, lives nearby and sees Johnny regularly. But we all know that this arrangement won't work forever, and she worries a lot about what will happen "after she is gone."

There are many unanswered questions. Today, Johnny is happy and well cared for in his state-owned residence. Will that support always be there? What about Johnny's health? Research is only beginning to explain the toll that long-term physical disabilities take on an otherwise healthy body. What's next? Will my own health remain strong, so that I can be an effective, if distant, guardian? What burden might all of this someday place on my grown children?

A year ago, Jovan, my husband of forty-three years, died. Some years before his death, he had a stroke and, for a while, required a lot of special care. A friend asked me, "How do you do it? How do you manage?" Without thinking, I answered, "I trained for this moment for the first twenty years of my life." In truth, Johnny has taught me much of what I know.

The last years of my husband's life were, in many ways, long and hard—much as the first years of Johnny's life were. Those years reminded me again of the crucial contribution that good information makes to a fruitful life. The hospice staff taught me about Jovan's dying, just as Sibshops teach kids about living with a brother or sister with a disability. Knowing doesn't make it easier, but it sure makes you feel less crazy. (No one should have to wait forty years for information in either case.)

These last years have also reaffirmed those adult lessons I learned way too early growing up with Johnny. It's not just the knowledge that's important. You must also understand that:

- Everybody's got something to deal with. If they don't, they've been denied the chance to wrestle with life.
- Everything you know and love and depend on can be swept away in an instant.
- It's all about managing your own expectations.
- It's all about living in the present moment and enjoying the gifts before you.
- Forgiveness needs to be a big part of your life. Practice forgiving yourself every day.
- The chaos never goes away. You have to learn to trust the universe.

I go to visit Johnny regularly now. He used to come to visit me, but age has made his care more difficult and traveling much harder. When mother is no longer nearby, I will have to be even more vigilant. It will mean more trips to Rochester. I am boning up on the services that are available there for Johnny and his changing needs. I am expanding my Rolodex, or should I say, my Outlook files. Mother and I continually check to be sure that all the legal and financial documents necessary for Johnny's welfare remain current.

With longevity running in our genes, Johnny and I may still have many years together. There are few shortcuts in this journey, but Johnny and I will work it out. We've done it before, and I am determined that we will do it again. It's about trusting the universe.

* * *

Kitty Porterfield *is the former director of community relations for Fairfax County Public Schools (VA) in the metropolitan Washington, D.C., area, where her work received numerous regional and national awards. She is coauthor of* Why School Communications Matters, *a book for school leaders about school-community relations, and is a partner in the firm Porterfield & Carnes Communications. Kitty has previously written about her experiences as a sibling for association publications and occasionally speaks to groups of parents, health professionals, and other siblings. A long-time resident of northern Virginia, Kitty is the mother of three grown children and the proud grandmother of five, with whom she plays basketball, bakes cookies, and goes to the theater.*

39.
Saying Goodbye to Jack

Mary McHugh

All around me the voices rise, loud and joyful, each one in a different key. The little chapel is filled with the sound of the residents of the Duvall Home for Retarded Adults singing a resounding goodbye to my brother Jack. "Amazing Grace," they sing, "Who once was lost but now is found."

There's a framed picture of Jack on the altar, taken when he was thirty-seven and first went to live at Duvall thirty-five years ago. He was handsome, blond, smiling, and you would not have known that he belonged in a home for the retarded, as they were called then. I love him now, but for most of my life I pretended to love him.

He wasn't so different from other children at first, just a little blond boy whose hands and feet turned in. We had our picture taken every year in front of the grandfather clock in our living room and there we are still, the little girl with curls and blue eyes and a sad expression, and the little boy with white-blond hair and a slightly mischievous look. It would have been unacceptable in our Scottish-German-English family to have admitted to myself that I didn't really love my brother, but I think I was an angry little girl who could never show her anger because we didn't do that. I think I was mad at my gentle, sweet, anxious mother because she had to spend so much time with Jackie. I think I was mad at Jack because he wasn't like the brothers of my friends. I think I was mad at my father who played golf and drank Scotch and hardly ever talked to me because he hid all his feelings. Like me. Like me to this day.

Bright and protected by my parents, I ran off to college, to Paris, to New York, to marriage and two children, always escaping into a life away from Jack. If you had asked me if I loved my brother during those years, I would have said "Yes, of course I do." What kind of a monster would I be not to love a person who couldn't help it that a mistake in the delivery room cut off the oxygen to his brain just long enough to derail his intelligence and change his life forever?

When I was twenty-one, studying in Paris, I sat in a little café in Montparnasse and wrote Jackie a birthday letter. "Jackie, you should see the French automobiles, " I wrote. "They're almost as small as the one you used to drive around when you were a little boy. Even *I* am taller than these cars, and you know what a shrimp I am." My brother loved cars and could tell you every Chevy my father ever owned when we were growing up. He could read, he could dress himself, he could understand you, but he would always be a child.

After I came back from Paris and met the man I would marry, we were sitting in an Italian restaurant in New York eating linguine with white clam sauce and I said, "You know, I'll have to take care of my brother some day." He just kissed me. "I love you," he said. "We'll figure it out."

Experts tell us that sisters of people with disabilities often choose husbands who need fixing because they've always been good at helping people who have problems. They marry alcoholics, workaholics, abusers, always thinking if they try hard enough they can change these men. If they're lucky and get a lot of good therapy, they realize you can't change people and pick a man who is strong and supportive and already fixed. I was lucky. I found a good therapist and a good man. And I never did have to take care of my brother because my parents set up a trust fund for him that made it possible for him to live in a warm and loving environment in Florida the rest of his life.

I didn't really figure out how much I loved my brother, how important a person he was in my life, how my whole life was colored by having him as a brother until after my mother and father died twelve years ago, and I was Jack's only relative. We were both middle aged by then, my children were grown, I worked as a magazine editor in New York. I took time off from my job to go to Florida to take Jack to Disney World, to Sea World, to a cottage on the beach. I wanted to get to know him. I was struggling to love him.

But it's hard to love someone you can't really have a conversation with. A grown man who clings to your hand when you're in crowds, who worries all the time that he is doing something wrong, that I won't love him if he doesn't eat all his vegetables. A grown man who says what he's expected to say: "Please." "Thank you." "No, I don't want any more." Polite, as my mother taught him to be. "Your brother is such a gentleman," the aides told me at Duvall. I tried so hard. "Remember how Dad loved to sing 'Home on the Range,' Jack?" I would say to get him to laugh. We both thought it was hilarious when Betty White in *Golden Girls* said she wanted to have her head frozen when she died. We ate lots of ice cream and chocolate cream pie.

There are so many kinds of love in our lives and they're all different. My love for my husband and my children is based on a kaleidoscope of experiences that are vivid and sharp one minute, quiet and steady the next, changing in subtle ways through the years, growing in infinite ways that bind us together for life. My love for Jack has always been a question mark. It never had the chance to grow and become stronger.

Then last year I found out my brother was dying of cancer. I went to Deland, found out how to take care of him, how to dress the gaping wound in his face, took him to a hotel for four days to hold him and tell him I loved him because the love I felt for him finally was so strong that I was determined to find a way to let him know. "Does that hurt, Jack?" I asked when I changed his bandage. "No, it's fine, Mary," he would say, but I knew it had to hurt a lot.

How could I help my little brother through this last part of his life? He must be scared, I thought. He must wonder what will happen to him. He must wonder about death. He wouldn't know how to ask me these questions. What could I say that would comfort him?

So one day, I put my arms around him and held him close to me and said, "Jack, you and I are getting older, and when you get older, you die some day. Do you know what I think happens when we die?" He looked at me so intently; I could feel his need to know. "What?" he said. "I think we'll see Mom and Dad again," I said, not knowing whether I was telling him the truth, of course, but I didn't care. "You do?" he said, and his whole body relaxed, as if he had carried this question with him through all the months of radiation and pain and wondering.

At that moment, I believed he would be with my mother and father again. That he would talk to my father about football and golf and what there was to do in heaven. He could tell my mother all the things he had been wanting to tell her all the years she cared for him. And I loved this little boy. I loved him so much my heart felt like it would break.

Jack died a few weeks after that, his beloved aide, Vicky, by his side giving him permission to go. "You don't have to stay any more, Jack," she said to this man who always tried to please. And he was gone.

The week after he died, I went down to Florida for Jack's memorial service. All his friends were there. They hugged me and said, "Don't cry, Mary; Jack's in heaven now." The minister suggested they all sing "Amazing Grace" for me. And they did, their voices rising toward heaven and my brother with a joy that would burst through the clouds and swing open the pearly gates, each one thanking God for the grace he had given them. And that he gave me that day when I loved my brother with a love I hope I can tell him about some day.

* * *

Mary McHugh is the author of fifteen books, including Special Siblings: Growing Up with Someone with a Disability, *the story of her life growing up with Jack. Her book was awarded a prize for Special Recognition of a National Project by The Arc of New Jersey. She served as President of the Board of the Center for Exceptional Families in Madison, New Jersey, for eight years. She has written about siblings of people with disabilities as well as her own story for* The New York Times, Good Housekeeping, *and* Family Circle. *Mary lives in Chatham, New Jersey, with her husband, Earl, a retired lawyer, and visits Mercer Island, Washington, often to see her daughter, Karen, and her three grandsons.*

About the Sibling Support Project

Since 1990, the Sibling Support Project has been a national resource dedicated to the well-being of brothers and sisters of people with special needs. The Sibling Support Project is best known for helping agencies start Sibshops—lively peer support and education programs for school-age brothers and sisters of people with disabilities. There are currently more than 225 Sibshops in eight countries. Additionally, we have presented workshops on siblings' unique joys and concerns in every state as well as internationally. SibNet and SibKids—the world's first listservs for siblings of people with disabilities—are hosted by the Sibling Support Project. Our other publications include *Sibshops: Workshops for Siblings of Children with Special Needs,* and three books for young readers: *Living with a Brother or Sister with Special Needs, Views from Our Shoes,* and *The Sibling Slam Book.*

To learn more about the Sibling Support Project, Sibshops, or our other sibling-related initiatives, contact:

Don Meyer
Director, Sibling Support Project
A Kindering Center Program
6512 23rd Ave. NW, #213
Seattle, WA 98117
206-297-6368
donmeyer@siblingsupport.org
www.siblingsupport.org

362.4 Thicker
Thicker than water :
22960000040369 MANF

NO LONGER PROPERTY OF
ANDERSON COUNTY LIBRARY

About the Editor

Don Meyer is the director of the Sibling Support Project, a Seattle-based national project dedicated to the lifelong concerns of brothers and sisters of people with special health, developmental, and mental health concerns. A sought-after speaker, Don has conducted workshops on sibling issues and trainings on the Sibshop model in all 50 states and in seven countries.

He is the editor of *The Sibling Slam Book: What It's Really Like to Have a Brother or Sister with Special Needs* (Woodbine House, 2005), *Views from Our Shoes: Growing Up with a Brother or Sister with Special Needs* (Woodbine House, 1997), and *Uncommon Fathers: Reflections on Raising a Child with a Disability* (Woodbine House, 1995). With Patricia Vadasy, Don wrote *Sibshops: Workshops for Siblings of Children with Special Needs* (Paul H. Brookes Publishing Co., 2008) and *Living with a Brother or Sister with Special Needs* (University of Washington Press, 1996). His work has been featured on ABC News and National Public Radio and in *Newsweek, The New York Times,* and *The Washington Post.*

Don is married to Terry DeLeonardis, a special education teacher and consultant. They have four children.